3 Rules to

Achieve

Breakthrough

Success

Table of Content

Introduction

This book is written with thanks to Peter Kyne, author of the 1921 "The Go-Getter". I was given the book some 10 years ago by one of the many mentors who helped shaped my life and success. Even when I read it all those years ago its examples were far out of date, but the principles timeless. Mr. Ricks, the "boss" of the story used the swear phase, "By the pink toed prophet." I Googled the phrase with no luck in finding out what it meant! The book discusses sending a message by telegraph and taking months to travel to the Far East by boat.

I was afraid Generation X and beyond would be at a total loss, and that they would not be able to benefit from the wisdom in these pages. I had a second desire.

After 25 year in the business of starting, operating, failing and succeeding in business I had developed a strategy to simplify the Strategic Planning Process, which is essential to any long term success. I decided to introduce that process, The New Rule of Three and honor Peter Kyne's work in the volume you are holding. Please enjoy "Achieve Breakthrough Success!: Introducing The New Rule of Three".

Chapter 1

A.P. Ricks and Company

Mr. A.P. Ricks was known in the Wall Street and investment world by "A.P.", short for Associated Press, because he always had a strong opinion and was happy to share it! Unfortunately, A.P. had more trouble than a Jedi on the Death Star!

He was happy to share that opinion in great detail with Mr. Skinner, President and CEO of The Ricks Financial and Trading Conglomerate, the Company that A.P. had built from his last two ten-dollar bills into a multi-million dollar success. A.P. was equally happy to share his displeasure with his son-in-law, Matt Peasley, the President and Managing Partner of Ricks Financial Education and Training Company, the second corporate entity A.P. had built from the ground up, teaching seminars and training people on everything from budgets to investing in the stock market online.

Mr. Skinner, thought of by some as "old school", although he preferred the idea of mature and reserved, looked on A.P.'s near tirade with his customary stoic demeanor. He had too much respect for A.P. and lacked any relations to temper A.P.'s occasionally quick temper. Matt, on the other hand, was younger and was family, albeit by law and not blood.

The young man leaned forward and matched A.P.'s glare with a fierce look of his own. "**Yooouu** think you have problems?!" Matt boomed, stretching the word you for emphasis. "Do you suffer from intense and constant migraines? Or have that joke of a Secretary of Commerce when you were in charge?"

"You can use that tone with me when you have surpassed 45 years on this earth and not before!" A.P. barked. "Furthermore, you know darn well it has nothing to do with politics and my health! What it boils down to is that, in what should be my golden years, I find myself surround by the greatest collection of over-paid, over-educated, under-thinking lay-a-bouts since Carter in the Whitehouse."

"Meaning whom?" asked Matt.

"You and Skinner, of course!"

"Why just what have we done to earn that colorful description?" asked Skinner

"You talked me into sharing my secrets, my way of investing, with every person who could scrape up a few hundred dollars and make their way to a hotel conference room. If that was not bad enough, you convinced me to open those hard-learned tricks of the trade to every Tom, Dick, and Harry with a laptop and an Internet connection." blustered A.P.

"Don't even get me started on the brilliant idea to have a trading office in every major city in the world. No sooner did we open those office doors and the last recession hit, the stock market tanked, and investable income dried up faster than a keg at a college party!

"Not to mention every Generation X man or woman we send to our Tokyo office starts reading their own press clippings, thinking they are the smartest investor on the planet, while taking huge unconsidered risk as if it was their God-given right, and believing it is their responsibility to drink every drop of Saki ever produced since the time of the last Emperor!

"In my old age, you two have forced me into the position of firing people by video conference! We didn't even have video conference when I started this company and now I have to use it to fire someone! And do you know why?"

Mr. Skinner and Matt took a deep breath and waited, resigned to the fact that their answer was not relevant to A.P.'s decision to continue.

"It is because we are playing on a field outside of our home turf. For crying out loud -- half our business is so far away we can't keep an eye on it, much less exert any kind of control when things invariably go bad!"

Matt, having reached his fill of A.P.'s rant, leaned forward, eye-to-eye, mere inches from A.P.'s face, and coolly stated, "We did not talk you into opening a service and educational company that has greatly enhanced the benefits, both real and perceived, of Ricks Financial and Trading Conglomerate. We talked me into it. I am the president and managing partner to your oft-not-too-silent partner's stake. I am responsible. You have nothing to do with it. As I recall, you retired ten years ago!

"Any and all trouble, difficulties or trials that fall on the company fall on my capable shoulders, as they have for the last ten years!"

A.P. leaned back in his chair, "Well that may be the case in theory, but on the practical side of things not so much. Seriously, do you expect me to check out mentally just because I don't sit in this office every day? I built this company. I can't sit idly by and let troubles destroy it or opportunities I see simply pass it by because you two are busy in the day to day operations. Surely you will not deny me passing input in a business endeavor to which I still have a controlling financial interest!"

A.P.'s face softened as he sat back in his high leather chair. "Don't misunderstand me. You boys have done a fine job running my interest the vast majority of the time. But Great Caesar's Ghost! What's the matter with you, Matt? And, no smug looks from you Skinner? You are in this up to your eyeballs as well.

"If Matt makes a mistake I count on your knowledge to catch that mistake and correct it before it manifests itself on our balance sheets or the Wall Street Journal! Matt, you should have done the same for Skinner here. Have you both lost your ability to interview and judge a man before you send him halfway around the world? If you ever had any such ability?" asked A.P., his blood burning hot again.

"You are referring to Henderson at the Tokyo office I assume?" Mr. Skinner cut in.

"I am Skinner, and if we had stayed in our own backyard dealing with solid American companies ... seriously, is Wall Street not enough excitement for you? If we had, we would have no Tokyo office to be worrying about!"

"First, the reality of a global economy is not up for debate." Matt stated with finality.

"Secondly," Skinner chimed in, "Henderson was the best salesman turned trader we ever had. In fact, he came through every position in this office from coffee boy to lead trader. I had every indication that he would rise to the challenge as he always has."

Slightly resigned, A.P. acknowledged, "I will admit we have to be global, there are strong companies and new ideas from virtually every corner of the globe these days. Henderson did do well here, but did you consult me before you sent him to Japan on his own?

"Of course not. I am the Ricks in Ricks Finical Education and Training Company aren't I?"

"The man was a week into his work before you shared your stunningly unrequested and long-winded free advice!" declared Matt.

"I told you he would not make the grade then and there, did I not?" A.P. asked, matching the younger man's fire.

"You did," Matt admitted.

"Well now, we seem to have time for me to share with you a little tale that you should have made time to listen to before you sent him out. Henderson *was* a good man," AP continued, a great performer, "when he had a better man over him. For the better part of 20 years, I had to remind that man not to read his own press clippings. Some days it was a wonder he could fit his ego into that corner office of his. Now Henderson has gone south with 100 million Yen from our Tokyo Bank account."

"You may recall, Mr. Ricks," Skinner cut in coldly, "that he was bonded for 2 million dollars, almost twice the amount in question."

"Not a word. Don't even try that. As you may recall, Mr. Skinner," A.P. said, matching his tone, "I am the genius that placed that insurance on Henderson, unbeknownst to you or Matt! I also remember being reminded by you, Matt, my dear son-in-law, that I was retired those 10 years ago and that I should refrain from sticking my gray mustached nose into the internal workings of your office."

Somewhat more somber, Matt admitted, "It was that foresight on your part that will keep the Tokyo office out of the red this year. The reality is that we have a serious situation here A.P. Henderson drank and gambled away everything he had and taken lines of credit he cannot hope to pay back just to do more of the same. In addition to not tending to business, he has run off with all the money in the company bank account! We certainly could not foresee this kind of behavior.

"When we trust a man to run an entire division, particularly a foreign division, that trust must be complete, all or nothing. There is no use in crying over spilled milk at this point," said Matt. "We find ourselves in the unenviable position of selecting Henderson's successor, who now has the double duty of rebuilding our reputation as well as repairing the mess Henderson left in the office. And we need to move on it soon."

"Very well, Matt," A.P said in his most magnanimous voice, "I'll quit rubbing it in. I am far from generous laying into you two like this. Perhaps when you have been around as long as I have and had to deal with people that have the moral compass of a sponge and lack that much intelligence, you will be a better judge of what a man can handle; just how much responsibility he can take. So Skinner, who do you have in mind for the job?"

"I regret to tell you," Skinner hesitated, "I have no one in mind. All of the men in my department are quite young … too young for this level of responsibility."

"What do you mean young?" A.P. blazed.

"The only man I would even consider for a job of this magnitude is Andrews and he is young, maybe 30 or so." Replied Skinner evenly.

"Thirty, really thirty is too young?" A.P. started, "As I recall, you were 28 when I gave you a $50,000 salary plus benefits and a couple million dollars in responsibilities."

Skinner began, "That is true, but then again Andrews has never been tested…"

"SKINNER!" A.P. almost choked on the words, "It is a constant source of amazement to me that I have refrained from firing you all these years. You say Andrews has never been tested. Why has he never been tested? It's like a car company keeping untested metal on the assembly line. How can you ever know what kind of car you will turn out? How can you count on it? Answer me that."

Skinner shifted and started to answer. "Shut it, not a word." A.P. continued, "You would have done this young man, the company, and me a huge service by taking a year off in the 80's when a baboon could have made a killing in the market. Andrews should have had his butt in your chair seeing just what he was made of!"

Skinner, seeing A.P. take a breath, plunged in, "Thank heavens I was not on vacation, as the bull market did not last forever. To say it was not easy to find the right investments to keep profitable at that time is a gross understatement," Skinner finished respectfully.

"Skinner, I cannot believe you have the nerve to contradict me!" A.P. cut in, "Do you recall at what age I turned Ricks Financial Education and Training Company over to Matt here lock, stock, and barrel? He had just turned 26. Skinner you are obviously getting old. It's fossils like you who have put a chokehold on industry and beat it near to death with ridiculous theories that a man must be old and gray before he can be trusted with an ounce of responsibility and a living wage. It's theories like those that have caused all our wars and strikes for crying out loud! The go-getters of this world are all under forty years of age. Matt," he continued, turning to his son-in-law, "what do you think of Andrews for the Tokyo post?"

Matt considered for a moment, "He will do."

"Why do you think he will do?" A.P. asked.

Matt continued, "Because he should be capable of it. He has been with us long enough to have the experience he needs to make solid decisions and…"

"Experience … experience, you two keep rattling on about experience like it's the end all," AP almost exploded, "It's courage and character that are important!"

"I know nothing of his courage. I can only assume he has some initiative and force of will to have made it to his current position. He seems like a nice enough fellow from what I have seen…" Skinner said.

A.P. interrupted, "That is not good enough! Before we send him halfway around the world I want to know if he has courage and that his initiative and force of will are up to the task."

"Then," Matt said with finality, standing to emphasize his point, "I wash my hands of the task of selecting Henderson's replacement. You have intruded to such a degree that I suggest you name the lucky man."

"Yes, an excellent idea," Skinner quipped. "I am quite sure my feeble skills and overrated experience fall short of those necessary to uncover Andrews' force of will and drive on such short notice. He obviously has the talents and abilities for his current position but…"

A.P., with trademark impenitence asked, "But will he have those same qualities when asked to make a critical and timely decision 10,000 miles away from expert advice, and the fortitude to stand by that choice? That's what I want to know, Skinner."

"I suggest, Sir," Mr. Skinner replied with a forced politeness, "that you conduct the interviews personally to ensure you are pleased with the result."

"I'll take that challenge, Skinner, and by all that makes any sense in this world the next man we send to the Tokyo Branch will be a go-getter. We have had three division heads go bad on us in that office one way or another, and that is three too many!"

Without a hint as to why, A.P. swung his aged legs up onto his desk and slid down in his high-backed leather office chair until he rested on his spine. His work-worn hands formed a steeple under his chin and his eyes took on a far away look.

"He is framing the interview for Andrews," Skinners said quietly.

"I know," whispered Matt. "I don't envy him."

"A.P.?" Skinner asked as they stepped out of the office.

"No. Andrews," Matt answered.

Chapter 2

The Meeting

The president emeritus of The Ricks Financial and Trading Conglomerate was not destined for uninterrupted contemplation, however. It was less than 10 minutes when his phone beeped, alerting him that his longtime executive assistant needed a word.

"What is it Carol?" A.P. demanded, pressing the intercom far harder than needed.

Carol Danver, having worked with for A.P. for better than 20 years, knew how to handle him. "There is a young man in the outer office. I have looked over his information and I think it is worth a few minutes of your time to meet him." Carol carried on, "His name is William E. Peck and he would like to meet with you personally."

A.P. sighed overly loud into the intercom, but knowing Carol was a fine judge of character and potential, eventually relented. "Please send him in."

Carol opened the large double doors and ushered Mr. Peck in with a gracious wave of her hand. The moment Mr. Peck came within a respectable distance of A.P.'s desk, he came to a stop at natural attention, reminiscent of a military parade stance. From a position that conveyed respect and confidence, he inclined his head to A.P., but it was the cool glance of Mr. Peck's keen blue eyes that held the much older, more experienced man's attention for long seconds.

Mr. Peck broke the silence but not his gaze. "Mr. Ricks, Peck is my name sir… William E. Peck. Thank you for agreeing to see me and for the opportunity to share the abilities and assets I will bring to your business."

"Ahem! Hum-m-m!" A.P. looked a little belligerent. "Have a seat Mr. Peck!"

Mr. Peck moved to take the seat in front of A.P.'s desk. As he crossed the room, the older gentleman noticed his visitor walked with a slight limp. A.P., being a quick and observant man, quickly deduced based on the man's age, his bearing, the American flag pinned to his lapel, and his limp that his visitor was a veteran, likely of Iraq or Afghanistan.

"Well, Mr. Peck," he inquired, somewhat more gently, "What can I do for you?"

"I have come about my job," the veteran replied with a slight, but obvious emphasis on the word "my".

"Great Caesar's ghost!" A.P. virtually exclaimed. "You say that like a man who does not expect to be refused!"

"You are quite right, Sir. I do not anticipate a refusal," Mr. Peck replied calmly.

"Why is that?" A.P. demanded.

Mr. William E. Peck's engaging but somewhat plain features rippled into the most compelling smile A.P. had ever seen. "I know The New Rule of Three, Mr. Ricks," he replied.

"What in tarnation is The New Rule of Three?" A.P. asked, somewhat confused.

"It is the simple truth that if you take care of the three most important aspects of any given situation, almost everything else falls into place."

"That sounds logical at least," A.P. said reluctantly.

"It has proven itself logical and capable of repeated success," answered Mr. Peck.

"Just where did you come by this New Rule of Three?" A.P. asked, attempting to regain control of the conversation.

"Do you recall watching Bruce Lee movies on Saturday mornings when you were just a kid?"

"Well, yes, but I don't see how that has anything to do with this," answered A.P.

"I watched them too, just maybe a few years later," Mr. Peck said with a sly smile. "At any rate, like many young men, I went to find a Kung Fu School. The closest I could find was Tae Kwon Do. They said I was required to attend one class twice a week, but was allowed to attend as many as I liked. Well, I like getting ahead and learning new things, so I went to two classes four days a week.

"I learned all manner of kicking and punching, blocks and falls. What I did not know at the time was that I saw my first example of The New Rule of Three."

"How is that?" asked A.P., a little more interested than he had expected to be.

Mr. Peck continued, looking slightly off A.P.'s right, as if seeing through the years. "My instructor said, 'You can overcome a larger, stronger opponent if you have solid technique and control of distance and emotion.' In martial arts, controlling distance is accomplished by where you place yourself using distance, and the angle in which you face your opponent. Being at an odd distance and angle, you force your opponent to constantly adjust breaking his rhythm, timing, and overall effectiveness. You begin controlling emotions with your own; you master your fear or excitement to reach a state of calm. From a place of calm you can taunt your opponent to anger him and keep him off balance; you can try and reason with them, or even stroke their ego to the point that the fight is no longer necessary in their mind. Of course you have to have good technique to make it all work."

"That is all fine and good," A.P. admitted, "but I am not sure what that has to do with our situation. You're a grown man now. You have served your country and are now looking for work."

"As a matter of fact, it was early in my career serving my country The New Rule of Three made its second unmistakable appearance to me."

"Do tell," A.P. commented dubiously.

"It was during Command Training, shortly after Basic Training, Tech School and Stint Training with the Army Infantry.

We were learning deployment of forces and use of terrain. Our gnarly old sergeant said, 'When confronting an enemy, how many sides do you want to attack from?' A room full of young Airman unanimously concluded that attacking from all four sides was the correct answer. The old sergeant shook his head and asked the simple question, 'If you are trapped by the enemy, what would you do?' Fight to the last man, we all agreed. Then the sergeant said, 'If you attack from three sides, you give the enemy a place to go.' He headed off further questions by adding, 'You control where they go, most likely into a position where they will be attacked from three sides.' So, again, by controlling three sides we actually control the outcome," finished Mr. Peck.

"I can see what you are trying to say, but what proof do you have to say it works?" asked A.P.

"It worked well enough to earn me a chest full of medals, but most importantly the respect of my men," Mr. Peck said again, briefly looking away from A.P. "When I left my last duty station, Yokota Air Base in Japan, my men gave me a replica Samurai Helmet as a thank you. The helmet was a symbol of leadership, and I know this for certain, only your followers can give you leadership, not rank and not position."

Returning his easy, steady gaze into A.P.'s eyes, he continued, "That's what I am doing; I am offering to put myself under the leadership of you and your team. Will you accept me into your ranks?" asked Mr. Peck.

"Son," A.P. said with a smile, "You win. When did you put yourself under the leadership of Uncle Sam?"

"The Summer of 1998, two short months after high school. My first trip to the sand box was the U.A.E. in Operation Southern Watch," Mr. Peck recounted. "In 2003, I had a few stripes on my sleeves and some experience in desert warfare, so I made my first trip to Iraq."

"That clinches it. I joined up to solider in the US Army in Vietnam. I made it through basic and combat training myself." It was A.P.'s turn to look back through time, "In fact I had to help some of my squad study up for the tests and drills."

A.P. returned to the present and his gruffness returned as well. "Wouldn't you know, an officer caught wind of it and said I was doing a bang up job. They needed trainers that could connect with the incoming troops. So I stayed right there at Fort Leonard Wood, Missouri while my squad went over to fight.

"I was heartbroken. I wanted to fight with my squad mates, but I stayed and trained. I know I should be thankful. The war was hard on a lot of folks. That was where I first started training and that lea us to today and to the founding of Ricks Financial Education and Training Company."

The story and kinship appeared to warm Mr. Peck's heart considerably. "I did a fair bit of training of my own men before I was invited to leave the employ of Uncle Sam due to the injuries I suffered on another trip he insisted I take.

"It was two years ago that I was given my Honorable Discharge, the GI Bill, $10,000 in cash and ½ pay disability.

"It was during the two years prior I spent recovering that I started to study business. With an injured back and left arm and new titanium leg, I thought I better make myself valuable for my mind and not so much the physical labor I could perform.

"Due to the grace of God, skilled doctors, and my stubbornness, or so said those same doctors, I stand before you certified to be of sound body and mind!"

A.P. looked at Mr. Peck with only slightly disguised admiration, "Not at all discouraged or mad at the world for your misfortune?"

Coming to near attention, drawing himself up to his full height, Mr. Peck answered seriously, "As you said, war has been hard on many folks, much harder than on me. I have my head, one leg, and reasonably good use of both arms. I can type, and even if one leg is titanium, I can hike longer and faster than most men given a good reason.

"So," Peck said, directly cutting to the heart of the matter, "Do you have a position for me?"

"No… No I have not," answered A.P. "I am out of it, you see, retired some ten years ago. The office is simply a benefit of owning the building. I generally use it to keep the occasional eye on the goings on, a place to pick up whatever still comes in paper mail, and mill over what I hear on the street and read in the Wall Street Journal. Our Mr. Skinner is the man you need to discuss this with."

"I have seen Mr. Skinner," the erstwhile warrior said, "but he was not altogether sympathetic. I think he came to the erroneous conclusion I was attempting to trade in my status as a disable vet.

"He informed me that there was not sufficient business to keep the current staff of trainers well occupied. I told him I was open to answering phones, making inside or outside sales calls, or keeping up with the emails. Although I will not likely make the basketball team, my hands reach and fly over a keyboard just fine."

"So, Skinner gave you no reassurance of any kind?" asked A.P.

"No Sir."

"Not to worry," the older man said confidently, "I will arrange a meeting with my son-in-law, Matt Peasley. He is the president and managing partner of Ricks Financial Education and Training Company."

"I also interviewed with young Mr. Peasley," assured Mr. Peck. "He was no more receptive." He seemed genuinely impressed with the certifications in strategic planning and group facilitation I acquired over the last two years. He said although he felt he owed me a job for my service and sacrifice, he simply could not make a place for me."

"Did he say why?" asked A.P.

"Yes, he said he was carrying a dozen veterans and did not have the heart to let them go, even though their productivity and business dictated he do so."

"Well, my boy, that being the case, why did you come to me?" asked A.P.

Mr. Peck ran his thumb over his combat coin, a token he had earned in the dessert; it reminded him that anything could be overcome.

"Because," impish grin spreading across his face, "I want you to go over their heads and give me a job." I do not care one wit what it is so long as I can do it. If I can do it, I will do it better than it has ever been done before. If I cannot do it and do it better than before, I will save you the trouble and embarrassment of firing me and resign myself.

"I will not be a charity case," Mr. Peck stated firmly, "I know I am not exactly the man I was, and that being two years out of the game is a bit of a disadvantage, but those two years of rehab allowed me a great deal of time to study business and why people succeed or they don't."

A.P. looked at the younger man appraisingly, "What makes you so sure you can succeed at a job you don't even know the title of?"

Full confidence returned to Mr. Peck's face, "USA," he said."

"We agree we are both patriots, Mr. Peck. I do not see how that is terribly relevant," A.P. declared, slightly annoyed.

"USA is the framework for the New Rule of Three, you see. It's an anagram," continued Mr. Peck. "It stands for: Understand, Strategize, Act."

"I am still not sure I understand how that matters here," A.P. said honestly.

"Well," Mr. Peck started, "The first step for me to reach my goal was to understand yours is the kind of company I wanted to be a part of and who in the company had the power to make that happen.

"Next, it was my strategy to arrange interviews going up the chain of command until I was hired.

"Lastly, I acted. All the best planning in the world is useless unless you act in a timely, organized manner.

"I have simply worked the USA framework and here we are," finished Mr. Peck.

"I see you have," A.P. cut in blandly, and pressed his intercom. "Carol, please ask Mr. Skinner to join us."

Mere minutes later, Mr. Skinner entered the room sparing a disapproving glance for Mr. Peck and turning suspiciously inquiring eyes to A.P.

"Mr. Skinner, old friend, trusted advisor," A.P. purred.

Mr. Skinner's gaze grew more suspicious as A.P. continued.

"I have decided to take your council on the Tokyo Office. We will have to take a chance. The office is being run by an assistant manager that will not make coffee without an ok from you, me or Matt. We have to get a real manager out there without delay. So here is the deal, we will send Andrews out on the next flight, but let him know that his position is probationary. Assure him that if he can not make a go of things there, he will be welcomed back in this office were he has proven himself very valuable," A.P. stated with his usual gruffness.

Mr. Skinner tensed ever so slightly when A.P. grew soft once more.

"In the meantime…err…I would take it as a personal favor if you would find a solid, productive use for this young man in my holdings. Do you think that would be possible, old friend?" asked A.P.

Mr. Skinner, in the vernacular of boxing and MMA, was down for the count and he knew it.

Young Mr. Peck knew it as well. He smiled as gracefully as possible to the president and CEO of the company he had just joined. He had been in the military and one of the first lessons anyone with any level of command learned was this: the commanding general's request was always tantamount to an order.

"Very well, Sir," Mr. Skinner replied coldly. "Have you arranged compensation to be given to Mr. Peck?"

A.P. threw up a deprecating hand. "That detail is entirely up to you, Skinner. Far be it from me to interfere in your day to day operations. Naturally you will pay Mr. Peck what he is worth and not a penny more."

A.P. almost whirled to face the triumphant but subdued Mr. Peck. "Now listen closely young man. Don't think for a second you have slipped gracefully into a good thing... I expect you to live up to your earlier statements! I expect you to step up to the plate and get on base, not only that, but I want to see the occasional home run.

"Everyone strikes out, but know this: the first time it's a warning, the second time you'll get two weeks without pay to think about it. If it becomes common, you will be off the team, permanently. Am I 100% clear?" A.P. asked, all but glaring a Mr. Peck.

"Yes Sir!" the military bearing returning, "All I ask is an opportunity to show Mr. Skinner what I can do. Thank you, Mr. Skinner for agreeing to give me that opportunity! To show my great appreciation, I will endeavor to be every bit as worthy as your confidence in me."

A.P. thought to himself, Is that a sense of humor on that young man? Poor old, by-the-book Skinner. If he ever gets a new or unconventional idea in that head of his… it may well kill him overnight. He is raging mad now because he cannot say a word in his own defense. If he does not make hell look like a summer holiday for Mr. Peck, I'll win the lottery on the way home and the whole situation will be moot. But Heaven help me how empty would my life be if I couldn't butt in and cause a little ruckus now and again.

Young Mr. Peck rose and turned to Mr. Skinner, falling back into his comfortable attention, "When should I report for duty Sir?"

"Whenever you are ready," Mr. Skinner retorted with a wintery smile.

Mr. Peck glanced at his well-worn watch. "It is 12 noon now. I will find some nearby lunch and be back here ready for work at 1 pm. I should knock out half a days work. He glanced at A.P. and misquoted Yoda:

"'If you quit your day now – if you chose the quick and easy path as Vader did – you will become an agent of evil and unemployed.'"

Unable to maintain his composure in the face of such levity during business hours, Mr. Skinner withdrew with his sub-artic dignity. As the double doors closed behind him, Mr. Peck's eyebrows rose in a sign of apprehension. "I am off to a bit of a rough start, Mr. Ricks?"

"You only asked for an opportunity,", A.P. remarked back. "I didn't guarantee you a good start! There is a reason why that is so. I can't.

"I can only drive Skinner and Matt so far – and no farther. There is always a point at which I quit... err... ah… William."

"More commonly known as Bill Peck, Sir."

"Very well Bill," A.P. slid to the front of his chair and looked meaningfully at Bill over his old-style glasses. "I'll have my eyes on you young man," he said sternly. "I will freely admit our indebtedness to you for your service but the day you get the erroneous idea that this firm is an old servicemen's home… " He paused thoughtfully. "I wonder what Skinner will pay you?" he mused. "Oh well, whatever it is, you will take it and say nothing. When some time has passed and the moment is right, and provided you have earned it, I will intercede with the old relic and get you a raise."

"Thank you very much sir," Bill said genuinely, "You are most kind. Good day."

Bill reached across the desk to give A.P. a firm hand shake and crossed the room with his slight limp.

The doors had scarcely closed behind him when Mr. Skinner reentered A.P.'s lair. He opened his mouth to speak, but was cut short by a wave of A.P.'s imperious finger.

"Not a peep out of you, my dear boy," he chirped amiably. "I know exactly what you are going to say and I have to admit you are right to say it… but I… well now Skinner listen to reason. How in the devil could you have the heart to reject that crippled veteran? There he stood on one leg with ¾ use of his right arm and a grin on his homely face that says, 'I will not be beaten. I will never give up.' But you, blast your cold unfeeling soul, turned him down like a drunk turns down a virgin cocktail! Skinner how could you do it?" A.P. asked with fire.

Undaunted by A.P.'s admonishing finger, Mr. Skinner stuck strongly to his distinctly defiant attitude.

"There is no sentiment in business," He replied angrily. "A week ago last Thursday, the local post of the American

Veterans of Foreign Wars concluded their employment fair for returning and disabled veterans. In just those 3 days you managed to find 209 positions in the various corporations and interests you own. The gang you sent to the call center in Dallas have already applied for a name change to A.P. Ricks Post 534! You had experienced men let go to make room for the veterans."

"You bet I did." A.P. yelled triumphantly. "It has been a resort for Generation X kids or millennials or whatever you call them. Asking for raises just because they show up on time most of the time. I am sick of unauthorized breaks and strikes. Great Caesar's ghost! Maybe these men of discipline, courage, and experience will be an example of how to work hard and be thankful for opportunity."

"I assume then," Skinner began, "Every office and shipping center should be run by a First Sergeant. I am thinking of having reveille and retreat play on everyone's smart phone, I am sure there is a bugle app for that! Or perhaps Saturday morning surprise inspections are in order. I will tell you this, Sir. The Ricks interests have absorbed all the old soldiers possible and at present those same interests are overflowing with the glory days. What we need are workers not talkers. These ex-soldiers want to spend too much time recounting past victories and not creating new victories in the arena of business!"

"Well our young Mr. Peck will be the last one I ask you to absorb… for the foreseeable future," A.P. quickly amended. "Have you read Sun Tzu's Art of War?"

"Not in years, I have been a bit busy keeping your company in the top 5," Skinner answered sternly."

"I believe it says something about a commander needing to know the strengths of his troops," answered A.P.

"Well A.P., Mr. Peck did not impress me. He applied for a job and I gave him his answer. He then went to Matt and was refused. So just to demonstrate his bad taste, he went over our heads and convinced you to foist him on us. He will rue the day he was inspired to that course of action!"

"Skinner, Skinner!" A.P. spoke quickly as if to head off a collision of some kind. "Look me in the eyes! Do you know why I asked you to take on Bill Peck?"

"I do," Skinner replied shortly, "You are too tender-hearted for your own good!"

"No you unimaginative dolt! How could I reject a young man that would not be rejected? I will bet you dollars to donuts he was one of the most dogged, tough, finest soldiers you have ever seen! He always carries on to his objective. He sized you up and did not allow you to prevent him from reaching his goal. He was opposed in the form of Matt and yourself but still managed to find a position here. That just might make him a go-getter. Plus he has this New Rule of Three philosophy that has sparked my interest.

"So, just what part of the dungeon are you going to place Mr. Peck in?" asked A.P.

"We seem to have an opening in the form on Andrew's position, with him heading to the Tokyo Office," answered Skinner.

"Oh yes, and I seem to recall we have six months left on that ill-conceived day trader penny stock training course that somehow made its way into our training list," stated A.P.

"Yes," answered Skinner, "along with thousands of pre-printed workbooks and follow up materials. You want me to put Peck on that? I thought you liked the boy. That is the skunk wood of our offerings."

A.P. continued as if he had just discovered a treasure trove in an old closet. "I want to see just what our Mr. Pack and his New Rule of Three can do. Let's just give him that to work with… you get my meaning Skinner."

Skinner smiled for the first time since he entered the room, a smile that would have made Mr. Peck wary if he were present. "And if he fails to make good with this chance… *au revoir*… eh?"

"I will grant you that, but I have a feeling he will do alright. I would hate to think otherwise," answered A.P.

"But here is the deal, if he does manage to convince people to pay for that… ahem… training and they get some good out of it, you have to give him Andrew's salary, office, and benefits. We must be fair, whatever our faults, we must be fair." A.P. rose and patted his General Manager's lean shoulder in a fatherly sort of way. "Forgive an old man's intrusions, but allow me just one more in this instance. Peck gets full control on the program, pricing, packages, hotels, the whole nine yards. If you work against him, I'll fire you on the spot. We must be true to our values. Remember, he left the better part of one leg in the sand."

Chapter 3

The Card

At 12:30, A.P. was hurrying down Congress Street to a luncheon at the Republic Grill, when he ran into Bill Peck, with his slight limp barley visible. The veteran stopped him with a good-natured wave and handed him a business card. "What do you think of that, up to company standards?"

The card read:

William E. Peck   713-442-7443

Ricks Financial Education and Training Company

Suite 107, 1001 Congress Street, Houston, Texas 77002

If it can be taught we can teach it!

A.P. ran a speculative thumb over the logo on the card. It was embossed, with the title of the company raised. This type of card had to be ordered and certainly could not have been made in the 45 minutes since he had seen Mr. Peck.

"I'll be dipped in branch water!" This was A.P.'s most terrible oath, never employed unless he was rocked to his very core. "Bill, as one bandit to another, come clean. When did you first decide you were going to come to work for us?"

"Two weeks ago," Bill answered with a wary grin. "You see, I applied The New Rule of Three to the situation, as I do with most important actions I want to insure are successful.

"First, I had to know 'where I was' and second, 'where I was going'. I was unemployed, but highly motivated. I started to research companies I thought I would be a good fit with and where I could make a positive and reasonably high impact. Once I identified yours, I had the 'where I was going'.

"With those two pieces of information, I could create my overarching goal, which was to become an outstanding employee of one of your firms, preferably in a training capacity, as training and leading people are my strengths.

Next were the strategies; during my research, I found that your firms were known for giving veterans a chance to prove themselves. I knew given that chance I could make good on my promises to work as hard as two men and earn my continued employment.

"I also found there were only three people that could put me in the position I wanted, so I started with Mr. Matt Peasley. When that was not successful, I moved on to Mr. Skinner, and finally to your office.

"It was really just the USA framework again. I had to **U**nderstand the situation, **S**trategize my approach, and finally **A**ct intentionally. The business cards were just a kind of visualization of my success. I had the stock created last week but not cut. So today, I just added the phone number and address and had them cut."

"And what was your rank when you went AWOL from Uncle Sam's good graces?" asked A.P.

"I was an E-5 Staff Sergeant," answered Bill.

"And no one offered you any better? You seem to have a bit of a drive," remarked A.P.

"Frequently; however, if I had taken the time to finish college and go to Officer Training School, it would have meant giving up the best job I ever had. You see," Bill continued, "I held two positions. First was head of Flightline Security. That meant every young buck that came to work on that flightline in the daylight hours was mine to mold.

"Don't get me wrong, we were all trained as well as we could be in Basic Training and Tech School. As Security Police, we received additional arms training as well as a stint of Army Infantry training. But that's only as good as the person teaching and the one listening. In places like Korea and the United Arab Emirates, things tend to be taken a bit more seriously.

"I finished my tour of duty on an Anti-Terrorist Team. It was responding with that team where I met with my less than thrilling career-ending mishap. I will tell you this, I saw that the situation was iffy, that's why I made sure I was the first man in. I am proud to say my team finished the objective and dragged my semi-conscious self back to safety.

"So you see, in both of those positions, I think I was doing things that saved lives. What's a commission compared to that?" finished Bill looking somewhat distant.

"Bill," started A.P., "Have you ever trained a roomful of people that want to get rich trading stocks without even considering the budget and discipline that is part of the equation?"

"I can't say that I have," Bill said returning to the present. "What is it exactly?"

"Well, it is a beginner's introduction to managing money with an eye towards investing," replied A.P.

"If followed, does the system work?" asked Mr. Peck.

"Yes."

"Does anyone ever take the class?"

"Occasionally, one of our bright young salesmen can scrape together half a conference room full of people willing to part with $100 to learn something – something they should have picked up in grade school if you ask me," A.P. stated with a sour look on his face.

Mr. Peck smiled, unconcerned, "I can sell anything, and for what it's worth, I'll teach the class as well for not one extra penny! Not even Skinner can have an issue with that."

Chapter 4

On the Road Again

For two months, A.P. Ricks heard nothing from Mr. Peck. The enterprising veteran had been sent to the Oklahoma, Arkansas, and Mississippi circuit. The quiet time from the field was a little longer than A.P. had expected. Then again, Peck was selling and teaching the courses in addition to locating and negotiating with hotels and all the sales aspects. So A.P. decided to give Peck the benefit of the doubt and allow him a bit more time.

It was not long after that when his trust seemed to be rewarded, as a large number of the Basic Trading and Budgeting Financial Workbooks began to stream out of the warehouse at such a rate that, at the four month mark, Skinner was in the unenviable position to ask for mercy and tell Mr. Peck to return to Houston to pick up the next shipment of workbooks and other updated materials and not set another class until additional workbooks could be printed.

With the need of new printed workbooks, Skinner knew the subject of Peck's success would come up in his upcoming meeting with his old friend. He decided to offer a primitive strike as he walked into A.P.'s office.

"Well," started Mr. Skinner, "I have to admit Mr. Peck has done far better than I had expected, especially while teaching the classes on top of setting them up. I will have a raise in his salary at the beginning of the year."

"My dear Skinner, why the devil wait until the beginning of the year?" asked A.P. "Your intense aversion to parting with money has cost us the service of more than one good man. You know Mr. Peck has earned that raise and you are a good enough man to know he will get it. Why not just give it to the man now? I want you to smile like you are in a Crest toothpaste commercial when you do.

"Mr. Peck will feel as if we actually notice and value his extreme work and the success it has led to, not to mention profits from a program both you and I had written off as a loss." A.P. continued, "As a surprising side-effect, Bill Peck might even decide you are a human being and not a Terminator bent on his total destruction."

"Very well," Skinner relented, "I will give him the same salary Andrews was drawing, as he did take over his territory."

"Dag-nab-it Skinner," a lesser oath sprung from A.P.'s lips, "You make it nearly impossible for me to refrain from reminding you whose name is on the letterhead and side of this building. Can you, in honest assessment, say that Mr. Peck is considerably more productive than Andrew ever was?"

"I do have to admit that he is, but you certainly don't want me to give him the salary of the instructor and the sales position?" demanded Skinner, trying to gain some control of the situation.

A.P. was momentarily taken aback. Skinner reveled in this rare occurrence, but was experienced enough not to show his pleasure.

"We must be fair," A.P. echoed his thoughts from months ago, "but we must be reasonable as well. What was the sales commission for that course?"

"We raised it to a full 30% due to its less that stellar appeal," answered Skinner.

"Hmm," A.P. thought for a moment." Let's give him Andrews' salary as you suggested, that will be a nice bump up alone. Then we will up the commission to 50% and that will still save us the majority of the salesman's salary, yet reward Peck fairly. As a matter of fact, seeing how you gave him the base salary for just one position when he was fulfilling the roll of two, let's backdate that commission to day one." A.P. glared at Skinner, waiting for an argument, but got none.

"Now hit the road. You are starting to make me nervous hanging around agreeing with me." Skinner turned to leave, as A.P. added, "One more thing... "

Skinner turned and stilled himself, "I assume you want a report on Andrews in our Tokyo Office? I was going to let Matt share that gem with you, but I will spare the young man the burden of giving you this report," answered

Skinner. "To quote Matt, Andrews seems determined to raise AT&T stock on his cell phone traffic alone. He calls at least three times a week on matters that are well within his authority and should be easily in his area of knowledge and experience. Your son-in-law is a patient man, and he has more grace than the two of us combined."

A.P. grunted in agreement.

"Even Matt has his limits and Andrews has found and surpassed them in short order," concluded Skinner.

"Ah well! I can't say I am overly surprised or disappointed. I am quite sure Matt will be in shortly to remind me it was on my great wisdom that we took a chance on Andrews in that post. I will call upon you to remind my young relation that I did, from the very beginning, state that Andrews' appointment was probationary."

"That you did Sir," answered Skinner.

"Well, I had better begin the search for his successor; it's the only way I will be able to at least soften Matt's cheap, but deserved "I told you so!"" A.P. was unusually quiet and thoughtful for the second time in one meeting, an event Skinner could not recall happening the past 30 plus years the two had work together.

"Mr. Peck has some of the leadership qualities I think would make him successful in our Tokyo Office. To make sure we do not have a repeat of the Andrews incident, he will need to be tested a little further," A.P. said with a mischievous grin on his face. He looked over at Mr. Skinner, "My old friend, I believe it is time for Mr. Peck to deliver a blue vase."

Mr. Skinner's stoic mask slipped and his features actually glowed. "Well," he said, "lets save the company some money this time and give the security company and the owner of the gallery a heads up this time." He walked to the window and stared over Congress Street towards Montrose Blvd.

"Yes," A.P. continued almost dreamily, "I think I shall give him the third degree." "And you Mr. Skinner, should our Mr. Peck deliver the... ahem... blue vase, you'll agree that he is fit and ready for the Tokyo Office job with the $200,000 salary plus all the bonuses and benefits that go with it?"

"I will," answered Mr. Skinner somewhat dubiously.

"Very well then," AP stated back totally in the present, "arrange that Mr. Peck has an open schedule starting at 1:30 next Friday and we will see whether or not he is a go-getter and how his New Rule of Three works under pressure."

Mr. Skinner nodded as he left the office, still chuckling slightly as the door closed behind him.

Chapter 5

The Task

Mr. Peck enjoyed being back in Houston and was just finishing his lunch at the local Chick-fil-A when his cell phone rang. It was the somber ringtone he had selected to apprise him when Mr. Skinner's office was calling. Sara, Mr. Skinner's longtime assistant, greeted him in her pleasant voice and went on to say, "Mr. Skinner is feeling a bit under the weather today, but does not want to cancel your meeting and asked if you would mind coming out to his home in The Woodlands to commence your business at 1:30." Sara conveyed Mr. Skinner's thanks and gave Bill the address.

Mr. Peck agreed and hailed a cab to make his way to the Skinner residence.

Promptly at 1:30 pm, Mr. Peck knocked on the front door and was ushered into the living room where Mr. Skinner was propped up with many pillows and several blankets. Mr. Skinner apologized for making Mr. Peck travel all this way and for the less that professional situation.

Bill thought Mr. Skinner must be on the mend as he looked reasonably well, but could only imagine how bad he must have felt to appear in anything less than a heavily starched button down shirt and suit of grey or black.

"Again," started Mr. Skinner, "I am sorry to have you come all this way. I believe the first order of business might make up for the inconvenience. Matt, A.P. and I have all been quite impressed with what you have accomplished in a relatively short period of time. In fact, so impressed that we are raising your salary to $80,000 and providing a 50% commission for each sale. How does that strike you?"

Bill did not try to hide the look of satisfaction that spread across his face with the smile that announced it. "I find that to be most generous and it is much appreciated."

Mr. Skinner began to ask about a number of details relating to the hotels and conference rooms, Bill Peck answered each one. At last Mr. Skinner sat up a little straighter and asked, "Just how did you turn this failing course around?"

"Well," began Bill, "has Mr. Ricks shared my New Rule of Three with you?"

"Only in passing," admitted Mr. Skinner.

"In a nutshell, it is the fact that if you take care of the three major aspects of any given situation, most everything else will fall into place," answered Bill.

"In the case of the Basic Trading and Budgeting Financial Workshop, the central question was why did a prospect not sign up for the workshop.

"Some were concerned it might not be worth the $100 price tag, others thought it might be a scam, and lastly some people thought they simply could not learn or use the information.

"Once I knew those things, I could devise a strategy to overcome the objections."

"And just what was that strategy?" ask Mr. Skinner.

"Now, I know in the past we made the workbook and all of the follow-up materials included in the price of the course… well, I decided to try it a little differently."

"I advertised the course for $50, but not only that, they did not have to pay at the time of registration or even at the door. In fact they did not have to write a check or swipe a credit card until the end of the training, and only then if they felt like it was worth the money.

"During the class, I emphasized the importance of budgeting, record keeping, stock research, and documentation. I told then how they could create their own tracking system with a combination of Word, Excel, Power Point and printed forms. I also told them for an investment of $100 we would provide them with specialized software with all the information and forms they needed.

"As you undoubtedly know, the vast majority of attendees chose to buy the software package.

"You see, when I removed the three major buying barriers by offering the pay after or not at all guarantee, I gained their trust, and that is all I needed. The material is quite good, and at the risk of sounding immodest, I am a better trainer than your average fresh-out-of-college, on my first job kid that was tasked with this material before," finished Bill.

Any retort Mr. Skinner might have added was cut short by the ring of the cell phone on the side table. Mr. Skinner answered the phone and listened for over one minute before he was able to cut into the conversation.

Bill sat quietly, trying not to pay attention to the call, until Mr. Skinner caught his gaze and gave him a small wave.

Mr. Skinner spoke into the phone, "I am so sorry A.P., I would love to take care of that for you, but I am not even in the office today. I have been quite ill… Thank you Sir, as a matter of fact, I am feeling reasonably better. In fact, Mr. Peck is here and we were just discussing his recent success. I could ask him if he might be able to assist you with this matter."

"By all means," Bill Peck hastened to assure the older General Manger, "always happy to lend a hand."

Mr. Skinner spoke to A.P., "Mr. Peck said he would be delighted to help you with this most important endeavor." Skinner carefully wiped the phone with an antiseptic wipe and handed it to Bill.

Bill started, "I wanted to thank you for this opportunity. Mr. Skinner just told me about the raise and I assume you had a hand in it. I am most grateful."

"Enough, enough," A.P. cut in, "You are getting just what you're worth. You won't get a penny more or less than that from Skinner or me.

"But as you are feeling so kind-hearted towards me, it makes my request just a bit easier. I was wondering if you might do me a favor this afternoon. It is too important to trust some delivery service and I doubt I could find one that could move so quickly as I need. I don't mean to make… ahem... a delivery boy out of you. As you can see I was going to ask Skinner to do it and there is only a handful of people I respect more than that sour-faced old goat. Don't you dare tell him I said that.

"What I mean to say…," stammered A.P.

Bill cut in mercifully, "Mr. Ricks, I have no false pride when it comes to helping out a friend or doing my bit."

"Great great... glad you are willing to plunge right in to help," said A.P. Last Sunday after church, my wife had me walking all over the city looking at Art Cars, bulls of all colors and designs, and every other craft under creation. I must have been in every indoor and outdoor plaza in the entire county.

"Don't get me wrong, I love spending time with the wife. I just prefer the air-conditioned variety. I did plenty of time in the elements during my stint in good ole' Uncle Sam's service. In fact, it is an old army buddy that has caused me to need this favor.

"You see, us old war buddies are prone to get together once in a while and tell war stories. They get more fantastic with each telling, of course. One thing this old soldier knows, it's that if the wife is not happy, no one is happy. That being the case, my buddy and I have turned over the planning of these get-togethers to our extremely loving and capable wives. In their infinite wisdom, the ladies have decided we would meet in Florida and cruise the Bahamas for the better part of two weeks. You know, a cell phone does not work on a cruise ship! I guess Matt and old Skinner will finally have two weeks free of my infernal interference. Bill, young man, do try and prevent them from burning the place down in my absence.

"As if the cruise is not long enough to be out of contact, the wife is insisting I leave my phone home for the 15-hour train ride. I do not know why we can not simply fly into Florida, but my wife has determined a train ride to be more relaxing."

Bill, concerned that A.P. may go on until it was too late for anyone to complete the unknown errand, interrupted, "Sounds like you have quite a trip ahead of you; how can I be of assistance?"

"Ah yes... down to brass tacks," A.P. answered. "It just so happens that on that Sunday afternoon, I came across a certain print from an artist I recognized. Now I do not know a Rembrandt from a Picasso, but my wife assures me that this picture of a blue vase with oriental scribbles all over it would complete the collection of my buddy's wife.

"As luck would have it, the store was closed. What kind of a gallery closes on weekends? At any rate, it is open until 7 pm tonight, plenty of time for you to pick it up and bring it to the Union Station Passenger Terminal. I'll be in car 17, stateroom 6. We don't leave until 9 pm.

"I would not ask this of you, but this buddy of mine, well as I said, we served together and no one can say for sure who might have saved each others' lives more times. He dotes on this wife of his and we are celebrating their anniversary on this cruise. Now, the print should only cost $5000 or so, nothing your new business credit card can't handle. I would gladly pay 10 times that for the original just to see the look on his face when he sees the look on hers. I will just have to make due with a numbered print," sighed A.P.

"I will do my very best to get this to you as soon as I am done here," assured Bill.

"Well, grab something to write on and I'll give you the name and address of the gallery," Instructed AP, "I just Googled it on this tiny screen."

Bill cast around looking for paper, when Mr. Skinner handed him a square napkin and a felt tip pen. With a nod of thanks, Bill wrote down the name and address as A.P. spelled it out for him, "Bradberry, b-r-a-d-b-e-r-r-y, 101 Montrose Blvd."

"Got it, Mr. Ricks… I will see you before 9 tonight."

"Thank you, Bill," A.P. said with as much earnest as he could muster in his voice.

As Bill touched the screen and handed the phone back to Mr. Skinner, the latter was grabbed by a coughing fit that actually scared Bill Peck. He quickly set aside the note and phone and went to his aid.

"Are you all right, Sir?" asked Bill.

"Quite all right, my boy, quite all right," said Mr. Skinner. "Now, explain to me again how you use this Rule of Three to help sell out the courses."

Over an hour and many questions later, Bill looked at his watch. "Wow it is after 5 already and it is an hour back to downtown in decent traffic!"

Mr. Skinner slyly removed his water glass that he had placed on the napkin note, smearing the felt tipped pen writing, and folding it to hide that fact from Bill. "Here you are, you will need this."

Bill quick slid the folded note into his inside jacket pocket and said polite, but hurried good-byes and went outside to await the cab Mr. Skinner had promised to call. After what seemed like an eternity, a Yellow Cab pulled up in front of Mr. Skinner's house and Bill began the long drive to Montrose.

Chapter 6

Bradberry's Bakery

It was 6:30 when the cab let Bill off near a plaza. The cabbie assured him 101 Montrose was just inside the central row of shops. Bill hurried as fast as his titanium leg would allow, and as the cabbie predicted, he found 101 just inside the second row of buildings. The only problem was, Bradberry's was a bakery and not a gallery.

Bill rushed inside and noticed a jovial man helping customers. Bill would generally approve of the time and attention to detail that Don, the baker, spent with each client, however, tonight he wished the man was a little less customer-focused. Of course, Bill knew if that were the case, Don would not have the line of customers that was so frustrating to him at the moment.

When it was finally Bill's turn, he tried to speak in measured tones but he was keenly aware of the minutes passing and 7 pm approaching.

"What can I get for you?" Don asked with true desire to serve.

"I am sorry to say," Bill started, "I am not looking for a snack. I was under the impression this was an art gallery."

Don smiled knowingly, "You are not the first one to make that mistake, although some call my turnovers a work of art!" Don paused, apparently this generally drew a laugh; Bill managed a weak smile.

Don continued, "Well you seem to be in a bit of a hurry. I believe the place you are looking for is Bradbury; it is in Vintage Park over in northwest Houston. It is a kind of artsy plaza like ours."

"Thank you sir," answered Bill, "I am sure your turnovers are quite good and I am sorry if I seemed short with you; I just have something I have to do. Best of luck."

Bill hurried back to the waiting cab. "Where is the painting?" the cabbie asked.

"Not here," Bill said. It seems I will be in need of your services a bit longer than expected. Are you familiar with Vintage Park in the northwest part of town?"

"Sure," answered the cabbie.

"How fast can you get me there?" asked Bill.

"In this traffic, an hour at best," answered the cabbie.

Bill slipped a $20 over the seat and said, "Let's see if we can beat that time."

The cabbie quickly pulled into traffic and raced towards the freeway. Even with the cabbie's Herculean efforts and a blatant disregard for speed limits, it was well after 7 pm when they reached Vintage Park.

The cabbie pulled to the front of the plaza, "Did he tell you where in this place the gallery was? It seems to go on for blocks."

"I am afraid not," Bill said. "I will just have to ask around."

"I would like to stay and wait for you, but my shift actually ended at 7 pm and I have a 45-minute drive back to base," the cabbie said.

"I understand," Bill replied. "It may take me a while to find this place and figure out what to do from there. Thanks for your help," he said as he paid the fare and another $20 on top for good measure.

Chapter 7

Vintage Park

Vintage Park outside shopping plaza did, as the cabbie mentioned, go on for blocks. Bill rubbed his leg to ease the pain as he made his way to the front of the plaza in hopes of finding a directory.

As Bill walked, he realized this simple errand had become a full-fledged project. A complicated one at that! It was time to apply The New Rule of Three.

As Bill always did when using the process, he would commit the plan to paper or digital media. He pulled out his cell phone and touched the note pad. He smiled for a moment at the fact that the app looked like the yellow legal pad where he had first jotted down The New Rule of Three so many years ago.

Bill shook his head to bring himself back to the present. This task was important and the more time that passed, the more difficult it would be to complete.

First, Bill thought, I must state my overarching goal, which is to deliver the print to Mr. Ricks in time for his trip. Next, I must understand the three most important aspects of this situation, which are: I must acquire the print of the blue vase; It is to be delivered to Mr. Ricks; There is a time limit.

Now, Bill was a believer in his own ability and downright stubbornness, and he would acquire the print. He would not stop until he did so. He would also make sure it got to Mr. A.P. Ricks for the same reason. The time limit was something that no amount of grit or determination could affect. With 8 pm rapidly approaching, the train station over an hour away, and the print not even in sight, it was the last aspect which concerned Bill.

He set that concern aside, as it was irrelevant until such time as he had the print.

Reaching the directory, Bill took a long breath in and slowly let it out. The situation was what it was, and a cool head would be better at sorting out the strategies he needed to achieve what he was now calling a mission.

There in the very center of the plaza was Bradbury's Gallery. Bill began his hike toward the center of the plaza and slightly smiled to himself. "At least this is progress," he said to no one in particular. He rounded the third square of shops and his allusive query finally came into sight.

Bradbury's Gallery: the sign was artfully done; the letters managed to swirl with stylish flair and still be legible. There in the window, just as A.P. had described it, was a print of an oriental blue vase. Bill had not been particularly fond of the picture when it was first described to him, but now it was a true thing of beauty.

Bill moved quickly with a slight limp to the front door. As he had surmised, the door was locked now that it was an hour after closing time. He looked around and found a doorbell. Without much hope of success, he held the button down for a few minutes with no response.

Bill thought fleetingly of breaking the glass and leaving a note of explanation and a promise of repayment. His good sense and a security guard that had seemed to have taken an interest in him loitering around the closed shop caused the thought to leave his mind as quickly as it had entered.

The appearance of the security guard brought a strategy to Bill. He needed to get in contact with Mr. Bradbury to procure the print, and the security guard might know or have an emergency contact for Mr. Bradbury.

Bill walked over the security guard, "Good evening sir," Bill started, "I was wondering if you knew the owner of this shop or if perhaps you could tell me which of his fellow shopkeepers might be able to reach him this fine evening?"

The security guard eyed Bill warily, "Mark, the General Manager over at the theater, is a friend of his. Mr. Bradbury sometimes sells the rare theatrical release posters Mark gets from the studios for charity. He will likely be able to get in touch with him."

"Thank you, you have been most helpful." Bill said looking at the theater in the distance.

"You look like you have been running around a bit, I could give you a ride over to the theater and get Mark for you," offered the Security Guard.

"Again," Bill said, "you are most kind and I will gladly take you up on the offer."

Bill Peck sat gratefully in the air-conditioned lobby of the theater, resting is leg, when the security guard returned.

"Mark will be with you about 9:15; he has to make sure all the movies get started without a hitch," the security guard informed Bill.

Bill thanked the security guard for his help and waited, knowing now that he would have to conceive a way to get the print, once he got his hands on it, to the cruise terminal in Fort Lauderdale. His musings were interrupted as Mark, the theaters General Manager, arrived.

"Good Evening, Mark Stanford, how can I help?" Mark asked, smiling.

Bill got to his feet and shook Mark's out-stretched hand. "I was hoping you might be able to get in touch with Mr. Bradbury for me. I know it is after hours, but I have a real need to purchase one of the pieces from his gallery."

"You seem pretty determined and like a nice enough guy, so I'll tell you what I will do. I will give Austin, that's Mr. Bradbury, a call and give him your cell number, and if he so desires, he can call you and you two can conclude your business," stated Mark.

Bill gave Mark his cell number and waited as patiently as he could as Mark spoke with Mr. Bradbury.

Austin wants to know what piece is so important that you would go through all this trouble.

"I need to buy the print of the blue vase he has displayed in the front window," answered Bill.

Bill's spirits were lifted as Mark gave Mr. Bradbury his cell number.

Almost instantly, Bill's cell phone rang. He answered, "Mr. Bradbury, thank you so much for calling."

"Well I would be a poor businessman if I did not even bother to call someone back that was interested in a $30,000 piece of art!" answered Mr. Bradbury.

Bill was momentarily confused and starting to be concerned. "I was interested in the print of the oriental vase, hanging in your shops window."

Mr. Bradbury answered somewhat less enthusiastically, "I was selling the print last weekend, and it was kind of a marketing campaign leading to having the original available. Should I take that to mean you are not interested?"

I would gladly pay 10 times that for the original just to see the look on his face when he sees the look on hers. A.P.'s words came back to Bill.

Bill answered quickly, "No, I would not say that. I just have to adjust a few things. I know it is late, but may I call you back in a few minutes?"

"That would be fine, I will be available for the next hour or so," answered Mr. Bradbury.

Bill thought about his business credit card; its total limit was $30,000. With the hotel rooms, flights, and meals from several months' sales trips, there were simply not sufficient funds to make the purchase.

Again, Bill returned to The New Rule of Three. First, does A.P. actually want to spend $30,000 on the gift? Second, where would he come up with $30,000 at 9:30 at night? Lastly, if he could find someone with the money, how could he get access to it in a timely manner as to convince Mr. Bradbury to make the trip from wherever he was to his shop?

Fortunately, Bill believed there were two people that could answer all three aspects.

Bill had not used either Mr. Skinner's or Matt Peasley's number before, but they were safely in his contact list.

He opted to try Mr. Skinner's first. It rang for some time before Bill gave up and assumed it was turned off for the night. That was even more likely the case, as Mr. Skinner had been sick that day.

With some trepidation, he dialed Matt's number.

"Matt Peasley, may I help you?" Matt answered.

"Yes, Mr. Peasley, my name is Bill Peck, you may remember you interviewed me for a job several months ago."

"Yes, Mr. Peck, I do recall your name," answered Matt, "but not from the interview. My father-in-law and Skinner have been raving about you of late."

Bill stifled a sigh of relief, "That's always good to hear. I have a question and a request for you."

"Straight to the point," interrupted Matt having been advised of Mr. Peck's test "that is one of the things they like about you. How can I help?"

Bill told Matt the story of the blue vase and the cruise with the old army buddy.

"So the first question is, do you believe A.P. is willing to part with $30,000 to make his old buddy happy?" asked Bill.

"Oh yes, those two go back further than A.P. and I do, he would most certainly spend the money," answered Matt.

"That, however, is not the point!" Matt said firmly. "A.P. should have never asked this of you. It is far outside your job requirements and he is apt to think everyone is his best friend and would do anything for him."

"Well," Bill answered, "he did offer me a job after you and Skinner turned me down. I am not claiming to be his best friend, but I hope I can be counted as a friend."

"I am sure you will be, but this is too much. It's late and A.P. is on a train bound for Florida. I can only imagine the instruction he must have given you. A.P. could not Google a good steak standing on the step of Taste of Texas! Bill, you have gone above and beyond in your attempt; go home and get some rest, A.P. will understand."

"That may well be the case," answered Bill, thinking of the bakery that was the first stop on his seemingly ill-fated journey. "But you say you are certain A.P. would want this print purchased and delivered for his friend?"

"Yes," sighed Matt.

"Great," replied Bill, "Now do you happen to have $30,000 lying around?"

"Not on me," Matt laughed. "Oh, you are serious! I can certainly put that on my card, but I am afraid I am entertaining some out of town business guests and cannot get away for an hour at least. Can you see if he will accept my credit card information over the phone?"

"I will," answered Bill. "And if he will not, I passed a couple of those payday loan storefronts on my way here. I should be able to get the balance of what my card can't handle. Let's hope for the best, now that I have planned for the worst. I will need your credit card information." Bill keyed the name, number, expiration date, and security code into his phone. "There that should do it. I will call you and let you know how it works out."

Matt returned poolside to his wife to enjoy the rest of his relaxing weekend, trying to not remember the details of his own 'Go-getter' test years ago.

Bill called Mr. Bradbury and asked if he would accept the credit card. Well, Mr. Bradbury, also being aware of Mr. Peck's test, started, "That is not how I generally like to do business with so much concern about identity theft these days. I would hate to miss the sale, but do you have any other options for payment?"

Bill sighed, "As a matter of fact I do. I can put $14,000 on my business credit card and provide the balance of $16,000 in cash if that is acceptable."

"That will work just fine," said Mr. Bradbury, "and since you seem to be on such a tight schedule, I will head your way right now. I will see you in about 30 minutes at my shop."

Thirty minutes, two cabs, three ridiculous fees, and four payday loan services later, a tired and hungry Mr. Peck stood waiting for Austin Bradbury, who arrived just on time at his shop.

"I know it is very late and I just wanted to thank you for coming down and opening up the shop," said Bill earnestly.

"Well, as I said," Mr. Bradbury continued, "I would be a poor business owner to pass up such a nice sale for the inconvenience of a trip down here. Might I ask why this purchase could not wait for Monday?"

"I am actually getting it for my new employer, you see. He is giving it as a gift to an old and dear friend and it must be delivered to him by 9am tomorrow." answered Bill.

"That being the case, let's get inside and let me get that picture framed and wrapped up for you," said Mr. Bradbury.

With painstaking care and what Bill Peck believed to be an extraordinary long time, Mr. Bradbury took the art from its display and framed and wrapped it in colorful gift paper. "How does that look?"

"Wonderful," Bill said truthfully, but biting his tongue to avoid allowing his frustration and fatigue to explode from his lips onto this man who had done him a favor. Bill bid the shopkeeper a good night and retired to a nearby Starbucks.

Once he found a relatively quiet corner, he thought of what he was trying to accomplish. The more time that passed the more difficult it would be to complete.

His overarching goal was to deliver the print to Mr. Ricks in time for his trip.

That had not changed; as well thought out goals tend not to change. The first major aspect was to acquire the print of the blue vase. With considerable difficulty, he had managed that goal.

He began to think of the second aspect, which was to deliver the beautifully wrapped package to Mr. Ricks.

Before he could settle or even focus on the issue, the smell of coffee and freshly baked lemon cake reminded him that lunch was some 10 hours ago. He decided the night was likely to be even longer and he could do with a strong cup of coffee and a slice of lemon cake.

Two slices of lemon cake and three Grande's later, a slightly refreshed Bill reminded himself that there was a time limit.

Chapter 8

Day or Night

Bill quickly Googled the airports, knowing a bus or train could not hope to catch up with Mr. Ricks' train that had left hours before. There was one red-eye flight left going out to Florida in about an hour, but the time and lack of funds made it impossible to consider seriously.

Knowing he must travel by air, Bill began to think of all the people he had met since he arrived in Houston. He had made many friends and contacts in his classes; the problem was they were in the surrounding states where he had taught the classes.

He thought of David Parr, who was in New Orleans. He was in one of the first classes Bill had taught. Months later, he had emailed Bill thanking him for what he had learned. With the budgeting skills and a fair amount of success, he had been able to avoid selling the small private plane his father had left him. A ray of hope pierced Bill's rapidly darkening mood as he scrolled through old emails on his phone. There it was, on the fifth line of Mr. Parr's email, after many perfuse thanks, the line Bill hoped he had remembered correctly. *If there is anything I can do for you do not hesitate to call day or night!*

As Bill dialed the cell number in the signature block of the email, he hoped David had meant what he said.

"What, hello?" a sleepy Mr. Parr answered.

"David Parr, Bill Peck here from the financial training course you took a while back; do you remember me?"

"Yes of course," a somewhat more awake David said.

"I am sorry to be calling at such a later hour, but you did say I could call on you day or night if I had a need." Bill said with genuine regret, "I have to be in Fort Lauderdale, Florida no later than 7:30 am."

"That is possible, and I am a man of my word. I will use any excuse to fly. You did help me save this very plane. I remember the hours my dad and I spent together when he was teaching me to fly," recalled Mr. Parr. "Where are you now? I'll pick you up."

"That might be a problem," Bill said with a weary grin touching his tired face. "I am in Houston. What is the latest we can take off and make it to Florida by 7:30 am?"

"Well if you can get here within three hours, we can make this happen. In the meantime, I will file a flight plan and get everything ready," answered Mr. Parr.

"Great, thank you so much for your help, I will call you as soon as I know how I am getting to you."

Bill slipped the phone back onto his belt clip. He pulled his combat coin from his pocket and began to play it across his fingers as he often did when he needed to think. It glinted in the café's dim light and apparently caught the attention of a young lady at the next table.

She pushed her long, black hair behind her ear, out of her pretty face, and asked, "What's that?"

"It is a combat coin," Bill answered. "It is kind of a special unofficial award or token. You see, combat units in the military will create a coin and only members of that unit can get them. It is kind of a way to honor your unit even if you're not in the service anymore. It was started by the Special Forces guys, but now a lot of the combat units do it."

"That is kinda cool," she answered, "but what do you do with it?"

"A tradition has sprung up; you can walk into a club and you lay your coin down on the bar. Anyone from your unit or branch of the service that is there has to lay his or her coin down or buy you a drink. I am easy, I just drink cokes," answered Bill.

"The catch is, if they have their coin and they lay it on the bar, you have to buy them a drink. So you have to be careful that you have enough money to buy drinks. It is a way to instantly build some friendship and comradely. Just make sure you never lay a coin at a VFW Hall, those old soldiers always have their coins…"

"That's it!" Peck said, literally jumping from his seat. "I could kiss you, but that would likely get me arrested!" He pulled $5 from his pocket and laid it by the young lady's coffee. "The next one is on me." He gathered up the package and rushed out of Starbucks, leaving a bewildered dark-haired girl behind.

Chapter 9

The Veterans of Foreign Wars (VFW) Hall

Even at this late hour, as the cab pulled up the VFW Hall, music and light spilled from the door as a patron entered the hall.

"Instant friendship and comradely," thought Bill as he paid the cabbie and headed for the door. Bill saw about 30 men and women as he entered. He walked over to the counter and with a loud "ahem!" and a flourish, he slapped his combat coin on the bar.

As he expected, more than 20 coins landed near his within seconds, accompanied with cheers and a few gasps of surprise.

"Beers all around?" he asked to a loud cheer.

Once everyone had received their drink, Bill took his coke and with mild difficulty climbed to stand on a stool. The room quieted down for the upcoming toast.

"First, I would like to thank all of you that served as I did in defense of this great nation. We all paid a price. Here is to those that paid the ultimate price." He raised his glass high and the room followed suit.

"Before you get back to being rowdy, I am looking for a helo jockey, so if you flew helicopters or know someone that does, please walk on over and say hello."

Most of the crowd went back to their drinks, but one man did amble over to Bill and offered him a hand in dismounting the stool.

"Name's Mark Hall." he said. "I wondered why, other than plain generosity, you would lay a coin down in a room full of hardcore vets," he said with a small smile.

"I meant every word of that toast, but I did think I might be able to find a pilot here," admitted Bill. "Did I accomplish that in you, Mr. Hall?"

"I am afraid not," Mark said; then seeing Bill's face fall, he continued, "My best friend, however, is a pilot. He operates a tour service called Night Flights. He is very proud of the name, obviously. He takes tourists on an aerial tour of the city after dark; it's a good gig and crazy busy at Christmas time. When did you need to fly?"

Bill shook his head, at the sheer sound of his next words. "Tonight"

"Tonight?" Mark asked, slightly shocked. "Where are you headed?"

"New Orleans."

"That's not too far by helicopter," Mark said. Mark looked at his watch, "You are in luck. Peter, Peter Kyne, is my friend, and he should still be at his hanger. Let me give him a call."

Peter agreed to meet Bill at his hanger 30 minutes later. As Bill paid his cabbie for this never-ending night, he thought he might be subsidizing the entire city taxi industry.

Peter stepped out to meet Bill and greeted him with a firm handshake. "Capt. Kyne, I understand you are in a bit of a bind."

"Yes Sir," Bill answered. "I need to be in New Orleans by 3 am, can you help out another airman?"

"I was done for the night and that is a bit off my usual flight path," Peter waved to cut off Bill's further pleas. "But from what I have heard, you have had a tough night."

"Thank you for considering it and I will obviously pay for a tour, plus the cost of additional fuel." Seeing a Houston Texans football team sticker on both Mark's helmet and the door of his chopper, Bill added, "I believe I can get you two tickets to my employer's luxury box opening day at Reliant Stadium, if you can get me there by 3 am."

Mark patted the door of his well-polished machine. "She is not as fast as the ghost I flew over the sand, but we will take that challenge! You relax here while I file a flight plan."

Bill sank down into a lawn chair near the hanger. His exhaustion competed with the hope that he could indeed complete what had become a mission as difficult as many he had under taken in uniform.

Mere minutes later, the two were winging their way across Texas. They shared an easy trip, each telling war stories in turn, but for Bill, time passed too quickly.

They set down at the small runway where David Parr had directed them.

"Here is my business card and my credit card info, just email me with the additional fuel cost and run that card Monday afternoon as we agreed," Bill reminded Peter.

"Will do," said Peter, "and good luck on the rest of your journey!"

Chapter 10

Air Borne

David Parr was standing outside his plane when Bill approached, his limp more pronounced from overuse and being cramped up for the long helo ride.

"Bill," I must say, "you have looked better."

Bill answered with a weak smile, "So long as you beat a departing ship this fine morning, I will be great regardless of what I look like!"

"Then get on board and let's make that happen!" David answered with what Bill thought was an obscene amount of cheerfulness for this time of the morning.

Bill climbed onboard and was delighted to see the older plane had a co-pilot area with ample legroom and a comfortable looking seat. He closed his eyes to prepare himself to listen and share those war stories again. He opened his eyes, momentarily blinded by the glare of the sun, and was surprised to see water.

David chuckled, "You fell asleep before I made it off the runway. I figured you needed the rest."

"I did?" asked Bill.

"I am not sure how much rest you actually got. You thrashed around quite a bit; what were you dreaming about?" inquired David.

Bill smiled a weary smile, "I was in a taxi cab that came alive and we were chasing a blue vase that had grown legs and a determination not to be caught."

"Well the good news is, we are actually ahead of schedule. With you out like a light, I flew a little faster; more turbulence, but I doubt the second coming was going to wake you. I will have you on the ground at 7:30 am, which gives you an hour and a half to find your boss and give him the monstrous blue vase."

"To be honest, I will be thrilled to hand it over," Bill admitted. They finished the flight in an easy silence, each man to his thoughts. David called the tower once they were in range and ask that a cab be standing by for Mr. Peck.

Bill found his way to the cab after a firm handshake that turned into a hug when David refused any payment. "I told you in that email that if it wasn't for what I learned from you, I would not even have her to fly in!"

Directing his attention to the cabbie, Bill said, "Take me to the Amtrak Passenger station… by way of an ATM, if you would sir."

"I'll be happy to," the cabbie said. "Should I assume you are in a rush as I was paid to stand by and be ready for you?"

"That you can," answered Bill.

"That being the case, and as you are my first fare of the day, I won't even start the meter until we hit the ATM, and even with the detour, I'll have you at the station by 8 am." assured the cabbie.

"Outstanding," replied Bill, forcing a much bigger smile that he actually felt onto his face.

True to his word, and with what Bill thought might be a disregard for law and safety alike, the meter started at the ATM and stopped at 7:59 outside the Amtrak Passenger Hub.

Bill thought a moment as he handed the cabbie the crisp newly obtained bills. "Perhaps you should stay; the way things have played out so far, I might need you. Either way, I'll be back in ten minutes to let you know." Bill carefully lifted the package out of the back seat and tucked it under his arm.

"Things don't really get hopping till closer to 9, so I have the time," answered the cab driver.

Bill quickly made his way into the station. There in the center of the lobby were the arrival and departure screens. He scanned the arrival to see that the train from Houston had arrived some 35 minutes ago on track 13.

He made is way to track 13 as quickly as he could, his fears confirmed. Not a passenger in sight. Bill looked more closely and saw the conductor and rushed over to meet him.

"Excuse me, Sir, do you have a moment?" asked Bill.

"Why I'll be…you would be a young man with a limp carrying a large rectangular package," the conductor said, clearly surprised.

"I guess there are not too many that fit that description wandering around this train station," Bill answered.

"I was to deliver you a message should I see you, which the gentleman in stateroom number 6 said was unlikely," the conductor paused as if for effect.

Bill paused as he was not accustomed to saying the type words that were filling his brain at that moment. "What was the message please?"

"Oh, yes, he would be at the VIP lounge at the cruise ship terminal. It is just five minutes by car," answered the conductor.

Bill thanked the conductor and hurried back to the waiting cab. "To the cruise ship terminal," he said, like he was giving the charge command to the cavalry of old.

The cabbie responded in kind, and almost instantly Bill found himself at the terminal. One more fare and tip later, Bill stood on his aching leg outside the cruise passenger terminal. The garishly painted signs and bright colors seem to mock Bill's exhaustion, but he steeled himself and entered the glass doors as they opened at his approach.

Chapter 11

No Ticket, No Entry!

The cruise terminal spread out in a large circle, with the outer most ring open to all. There were several check points, not so much security as much as entry points watched by employees.

Bill blended in with a loud group of travelers and entered the second ring. Here, he saw a flurry of activity. Porters in red jackets flitted around carrying bags, packages, and serving guests' drinks and snacks.

Finally, he saw the VIP area at the top of the hall nearest the departure door. It encompassed 25% of the entire building and had two entrances, one on either side. Inside, there were small shops selling everything a traveler could need from sunscreen and sunglasses to magazines and swimsuits. Two drink stations and a snack cart were all surrounded by the now familiar red-jacketed porters.

Bill opted for the direct approach. He had a saying, walk with purpose and people will often assume you are supposed to be there. This, however, was not the case for the attendant manning the closest VIP entrance. As the uniformed man stepped in front of Bill to block his way, he said, "May I see your ticket please?"

"I am not actually taking a cruise, you see…" started Bill.

"No ticket, no entry!" the man said haughtily.

"I understand that," began Bill. "I just need to find my friend and give him a package."

"No ticket, no entry!" The man said again.

"All right, can you page Mr. Ricks and have him come here so I can deliver his property?" asked Bill, fighting back anger, which was surely starting to show on his face.

"This is not Wal-Mart, our guests come here to board our ships in order to leave work and stress behind. We do not page them. If this package or you were so important, you would be able to reach him by cell phone or he would have waited for the package."

Bill opted not to say anything as he was on the verge of beating the attendant unconscious with his own titanium leg. He chose instead to walk away.

He sat down in a comfortable chair and laid the package beside him. Bill was perplexed as to how he could possibly have made it this far, overcome so much, just to be stopped by an over-dressed security guard with an attitude, only 100 yards from the room Mr. Ricks was sitting in.

Bill was jarred from his musing as the voice of one of the porters was informing people that VIP boarding would begin in 15 minutes and they had 45 minutes to make last minute arrangement before they could board.

The porter stopped in front of Bill's chair and waited until Bill looked up and made eye contact.

"Can I help you with your package, Sir?" he asked.

Hope flooded back into Bill's mind, which had come up with no other plan in the intervening minutes. "Why yes, yes you can!" answered Bill. "I need to get this package to Mr. A.P. Ricks in the VIP area."

"Certainly," said the porter, "May I see the label please?"

Bill's face must have fallen as he answered that it did not have one.

The porter, obviously accustom to making his guests happy, perked up, "Come this way." He led Bill to the opposite end of the building from the VIP area.

"Wait right here," the helpful man said. "Behind these swinging doors is the wonderful world of porters," he said, obviously trying to raise Bill's spirits. "With your permission, I will open your package and have my supervisor inspected it; with that, you will have your label and I will deliver it to your friend!"

"That's great!" Bill exclaimed. "How long with that take?"

"20 minutes or so to get the supervisor over here and everything inspected," answered the porter.

"20 minutes!" Bill sighed, "Mr. Rick boards in 10."

"Sorry, the supervisor just left to make his rounds, I could not possibly get him back here in 10 minutes," answered the porter. "I wish there was something I could do."

"I wish I were a porter, you seem to have the run of the place." Bill's swirling mind snapped into place. "Thank you for trying, I'll just have to get it to him when he returns." The porter apologized that he could not do more and left to attend to other guests.

Bill thought to himself, these navy pants I am wearing can pass for black and if I were to temporarily borrow one of those red jackets… Bill picked up the package and carried it in front of his chest completely hiding his shirt and most of his face and entered through the swing doors to the wonderful world of porters.

He kept the large package between himself and everyone he saw, until he noticed the lockers and a coat rack. There on the center peg was a jacket, just his size. He maneuvered over to it, slipped it on behind the cover of his box and moved out the door.

He moved as fast as he thought he could without drawing attention to himself, over to the second entrance of the VIP area.

As he approached the second entrance, he called to the uniform attendant, "Package for a Mr. A.P. Ricks," as if he were reading from a label on his side.

"Yes," said the attendant, checking his iPad and barely looking up, "You just made it, they are about to start boarding. He should be in section C."

Bill looked up and saw large letters above each group of very plush chairs. He made his way to the large silver C just in time to see Mr. Ricks stand to start the boarding process.

Chapter 12

Finally

A.P. almost turned right into him as Bill hurried towards him. "I'll be dipped in branch water! I cannot believe you're here!" A.P. said, staring at Bill as if he were, in fact, a ghost.

Bill pulled himself in as straight of attention his aching back and sore leg would allow. "I am sorry to cut this so close, I ran into a few problems…"

"Great Caesar's ghost! A few problems!" A.P. interrupted, "I had Skinner delay to the point it would have been hard to reach the shop if I had given you the right address to start with. It was Matt's job to try and discourage you, and with a price that was six times higher than you were told, that would have stopped most men by itself. I knew if you were able to retrieve it, it would be far too late to take conventional means to reach me here."

Bill listened with a mixture of shock and fury on his face. Only the bearing he obtained in years of military service allowed him to keep from lashing out verbally. The revelation that the previous night was purposefully done was much more than he could take, and he almost dropped the package as he all but fell into the large chair A.P. has just vacated.

He collected himself, adjusted the package securely next to the chair, and got back to his feet, trying to salvage what pride he felt he had left. "I do not begrudge a man a joke, and I am entirely grateful that you hired me against the advice of your two best men, but I feel you have taken advantage of me. You know I am a man that does not question the authority of a man I trust, that I complete whatever task I have been appointed. I have that tendency and Uncle Sam was happy to hone it during my time in the service."

"I believe that to be the case," A.P. said. "But let me ask you this, why did you not quit?"

"Aside from the reason I just gave you, I believe it is important to repay kindness with kindness. I guess it is because I am an honorable man."

"I can see you are a man of good reputation, from your action and the plentiful references on your resume," A.P. assured him.

"I spent a few years in Japan during my service, and they have another idea of what honor is," explained Bill. "In that culture, when someone does something or performs a task for you, you carry an *on'* (pronounced own) for them. That's an obligation. As soon as it is possible, an honorable man will repay that *on'* with a greater or more valuable task. It is not a way to out do each other, but to honor the each other.

"You took a chance on me when you gave me this job, and I felt like I carried an *on'* for you and this was a good way to repay it at least in part.

"Lastly," Bill said, "my mother and the Good Book both told me to do with your heart what your hands find to do." Referencing his mother and the Bible was finally enough to cause Bill's shoulders, previously shaking with rage, to still themselves, and Bill's breathing slowed to a normal pace as he sat back down.

A.P. reached over and ruffled the younger man's hair in a fatherly sort of way. "That was cruel – damnable cruel, but I have a big opportunity for you. So I had to find out several things about you before I entrusted you with the job."

"So," A.P. continued, "I arranged a 'Go-getter test'. You were under the mistaken idea that you were carrying a print of a blue vase all the way from Houston. What you were actually carrying was a $300,000 a year job, complete with bonuses and stock options. Your time in Japan and the incredible lengths you went through to bring this print have convinced me you are the man for the top spot in our Tokyo office. If you're interested, of course."

Bill looked up into A.P.'s eyes, trying to comprehend what he had just heard. "You are saying this was part of a job interview?"

"That's one way to think about it, and I will say you performed far better than could have been reasonable expected," answered A.P. "So the Tokyo job and all that comes with it is yours for your efforts!"

"I will be the best man you have ever sent to that small island and I will do my best to never give you cause to question your decision," answered Bill earnestly.

"I don't doubt it for a minute, Mr. Peck, and not because we have had a string of good men fail at that office. That post being so far from the home office has got the better of three good men. It takes a certain kind of something to handle an office on the other side of the world. That is why I needed a Go-getter to handle it, and with apologies, that is why you had to endure the Go-getter test. As a matter of knowledge, 15 men have been so tested and you are only the third to have completed it over all those years."

"I can not imagine leading any office to be quite as intense as the last 48 hours!" remarked Bill.

A.P. chuckled, "It is certainly a different kind of stress. I know now what I expected at our first meeting."

"What was that?" Bill asked.

"That you will always give every effort to accomplish your goal; that you never give up, even when the odds are stacked heavily against you. In short, I thought you were a Go-getter. I am happy that you proved me right."

Bill nodded. "That being the case, I think I can find it in my heart to forgive the indignation you heaped upon me these last few days."

A.P. could not quite read Bill's face. He decided to continue on as if he were joking. "I am anxious to see what you and your New Rule of Three can do."

Bill's mind had finally stopped whirling and he looked around. He did not see Mrs. Ricks or the old army buddy or his wife. "I take it there is no anniversary for an old friend?"

A.P. smiled, "I find it wise to be gone for a week or so after someone fails the Go-getter test. Mr. Skinner's smug look and tut-tuts make me pretty near crazy and young Matt walks on egg shells as if I will snap at anyone that dares come within ten feet of me. So I take a week to play golf or in this case, book a cruise."

"So you thought I would fail?" asked Bill, with a look of indignation of his face.

"I would not exactly say that," A.P. grinned as he reached in to his pocket and drew out an envelope.

Bill stared at the envelope as if trying to use x-ray vision to see what was within.

A.P. waited, allowing the tension to build. "You see, my cabin has two bedrooms; they can do the darnedest things on boats these days." He held the envelope out to Bill.

"That would be a first-class ticket to join me. I figured you might need a bit of relaxation should you actually make it here, and here you are!"

Bill, on the verge of being overwhelmed due to his exhaustion and the sheer amount and importance of the information he was receiving at such a rapid pace, finally reached and took the envelope. "I will be happy to join you."

"You might want to leave the jacket here, otherwise people might ask you to carry their bags," warned A.P.

Bill looked down and seemed surprised to see the red porter's jacket. "That is probably a good idea."

A.P. waved down an actual porter and handed over the jacket and the package.

"Wait," shouted Bill. "That is a $30,000 piece of art, you can't just hand it off without careful instructions!"

"Actually it is a $3 poster I had my assistant pick up at Michaels Arts and Crafts, along with the fake wood frame," answered A.P. with a somewhat sheepish grin.

Bill smiled, finally able to grasp the entire situation and let go of the negative emotions. "I should have known."

A porter walked up to them and waited for a break in the conversation, "Sir, you should be boarding. May I guide you to your cabin?"

"Well Bill, what do you say? Shall we get started?" asked A.P.

"Lead the way, Mr. Ricks, lead the way!"

Chapter 13

Bill Peck's Rules of Three

I hope you enjoyed the story as much as I did when I read Peter B. Kyne's 1921 original some ten years ago. That story was about becoming a Go-getter, but was more inspirational than instructional.

We live in a busy world and being inspired is good, but being inspired and given the tools to use that inspiration is even better!

Notice I said given the tools. Any coach or consultant that tells you they can change your life or business are either mistaken or have a far too great opinion of themselves.

Only you can change your life and business. As a coach, I will provide you with the tools to make it as easy as possible. I tell my clients that I can only show them the path and they must make the journey.

I will accompany you, guide you, and perhaps most importantly, hold you accountable, but that is all I can do.

I am going to share with you Bill Peck's use of The New Rule of Three in the same written format I use with my clients.

NOTE: We are all different in the way we learn and retain information. Some like to read examples, and then read the report fully detailing The New Rule of Three. Others like to read the subject matter first and then look over the example.

If you would like to read The New Rule of Three Report first, mark this page and jump to Chapter 14, then return here for the examples.

For those that have decided to go with the examples first, let me share this most condensed idea of what The New Rule of Three is:

The New Rule of Three states that if you take care of the three major aspects of any given situation, everything else tends to fall into place.

If we were to join Mr. Peck in the VA hospital recovering from his injuries, we would see him realize that his time in the service was over. As he always did, he applied The New Rule of Three to this very important decision: What would he do for a living now?

He asks the question, "What are the three most important aspects of a career?"

1. **What do I like to do?** He recognized a person generally spends about 1/3 of their life working, so likening whatever he chose was critical to a happy life.
2. **What can I do?** We all have limitations. Bill knew he had physical limitations he had to consider, but we all need to be honest with ourselves about

whatever limitations affect such an important choice.

3. **Can I live where and how I want?** A career must be able to provide for our financial needs whether it is just us or a family. A job, no matter how much we love it, that does not allow for basic necessities, is not a good fit. Where you live will often determine the amount of compensation you need. The cost of living in Houston is 5 to 10 times less than California or New York.

Let's explore Bill's answers to these questions.

> **1. What do I like to do?** Bill had always been a people person. He had enjoyed training new members of the Air Force so much that he turned down promotion. He knew the corporate world had a position for trainers and if he found a company whose ideas he agreed with, he could feel great about teaching those ideals and helping new people fit into the company's culture. He could say with certainty, **that is something I would like to do**.

> **2. What can I do?** Bill thought about his training and experience in the field of training and instruction. From an intellectual point of view, Bill was sure he could do it. The doctors assured him that with rehabilitation and practice, he would have 60% capability and use with an artificial leg. Bill

knew he would beat that, but decided that the ideal job would not require him to stand for more that 6 hours at a time and would allow for breaks so he could rest. Bill, with reasonable certainty, said, **I can do this.**

3. Can I live where and how I want? Bill knew he had always preferred warmer climates, and after speaking with other amputees who had warned him that big shifts in weather caused them discomfort, Bill decided to look into the southern states. After researching, he found Texas to have the strongest economy in the US. In Texas, Houston was in the top 5 on virtually every list of best business climates in the US he could find. Houston also had a huge population of oil and gas businesses and the sprawling support sector from manufacturing to service companies. These companies would provide a target rich environment for a job search as a training candidate. The cost of living was lower than most major cities in other parts of the country, so a salary could be lower and still afford a good standard of living. So with all those things considered, Bill said, **I can live how I want and where I want with this job.**

Here is a summary of Bill's answers to the question: What are the three most important aspects of choosing a career?

1. **What do I like to do?** I would like to be a trainer in a corporate atmosphere.
2. **What can I do?** Yes, I can be a trainer in a corporate setting.
3. **Can I live where and how I want?** Yes, I can live in Houston and live well on the average salary of a trainer in Houston.

The use of The New Rule of Three provided Bill a filter to reduce the literally millions of job choices to a reasonable number that were right for him. Your answers would and should be different to the same questions.

Based on the choices Bill made, he knew he was looking for a corporate training position in Houston, TX. With that knowledge, he was able to concentrate his search in Houston, where he would eventually apply The New Rule of Three again.

The question this time was what company would offer the best opportunity for Bill to acquire a training position.

The first consideration was to find a company that had training as one of its main activities.

Second, is the phase of the company, was it in a stable or growth phase.

Third, in Bill's case, did they have a preference or history of hiring veterans.

This set of questions is more than just a consideration on Bill's part. They require action, and effective action almost always requires planning. Fortunately, the New Rule of Three philosophy includes a simple, yet effective, planning system.

Chapter 14

The Plan

The overarching goal for Bill's plan was:

To find a stable or growing company that had training as a major activity in the city of Houston and had veteran friendly hiring policies.

The first strategic goal would be to:

1) Create a list of companies that fit that profile

The action items for this strategic goal were:

A) Pick up a subscription to the Houston Business Journal and get the Book of Lists. The book contained the top 100 businesses in all types of categories, including the top executive's contact information.
Who: Bill Peck   Start: Jan. 1, 2013   Complete: N/A   Outside Cost: $50

B) Use Monster and Houston Employment Weekly to create a list of the top 10 firms hiring.
Who: Bill Peck   Start: Jan. 1, 2013   Complete: Jan. 7, 2013

C) Speak to the local VA and personally network at VFW to see if the   companies on his list had a tendency to hire veterans.

Who: Bill Peck   Start: Jan. 7, 2013   Complete: Jan. 21, 2013

The second strategic goal would be:

2) **Research each of the 10 companies that met the criteria stated in the over-arching goals.**

The action items for this strategic goal were:
   A) **Read the entire website of all 10 companies. Who: Bill Peck   Start: Jan. 21, 2013 Complete: Jan. 28, 2013**

   B) **Search for press releases, both positive and negative, on the listed businesses. Who: Bill Peck   Start: Jan. 21, 2013 Complete: Jan. 28, 2013**

   C) **Find where rank and file employees tend to have lunch and observe and speak to current employees. Who: Bill Peck   Start: Jan. 28, 2013 Complete: Feb. 5, 2013**

The third strategic goal would be:

3) **Choose the top three companies that fit the profile and check out the leaders and hiring managers of those firms.**

The action items for this strategic goal were:

A) Identify the top leaders of selected companies.
Who: Bill Peck   Start: Feb. 5, 2013
Complete: Feb. 8, 2013

B) Research those leaders to determine hiring preferences and areas of common interest.
Who: Bill Peck   Start: Feb. 8, 2013
Complete: Feb. 12, 2013

C) Find contact information for the key leaders and hiring managers.
Who: Bill Peck   Start: Feb. 12, 2013
Complete: Feb. 15, 2013

Bill started with an infinite number of possible jobs and locations to consider, but using the New Rule of Three, he narrowed his search to:

1) A company that had training as a major activity
2) A company located in Houston, TX
3) A company that had hiring preferences for veterans.

While much more focused, this still left Bill with too many opportunities to research every one.

In order to fine-tune his search, he selected the top 10 firms that met his criteria or filter to meet his needs. From that 10, he selected the top 3 on which to concentrate.

With this impossible mass of possibilities narrowed down to the top 3 for his specific need, Bill was able to do in-depth research on the people that would most likely give him what he needed.

As you can see, the strategic planning portion of The New Rule of Three Philosophy is based on carefully choosing three overarching goals. Those goals are now subjected The New Rule of Three or TNRO3.

The question is: What are the three most important strategies to make that goal a reality? These three strategic goals will support the overarching goal.

Each of the three strategic goals will be supported by 3 to 5 action items. In this format, we create a simple cause and effect dynamic.

When these three action items are done/completed/happen, then this strategic goal will be completed. If all three strategic goals are done/completed/happen, then the overarching goal will become a reality.

This is only true if you put a great deal of thought and research into making the goals at each level. As important as the goals themselves are, the action items are critical to making it all happen.

In TNRO3, action items are much more than a to-do list. As you saw in Bill's plan, every action item has a start date, as well as a completion date if appropriate. Beyond that, it is assigned to a specific person. In Bill's case, he was working alone, so he was assigned all the action items or tasks. Lastly, if there is an outside cost, a cost other than the standard labor and supplies used by the person responsible for that task, then that extra cost needs to be accounted for in your strategic plan.

Assigning the action item to the right person is very important; it must match their skills and abilities. The benefit to the leader crafting the plan is accountability.

One of my chief complaints with some strategic plans is that they are too long and complicated to use on a regular basis.

With the start, completion time, and a name of who is responsible on every action item, a leader can quickly determine from whom and when they need an update. It becomes a simple question: "Mr. Smith, have you started on task X, and are you on track to have it completed by date X?"

If the answer is an honest yes, nothing more is required, otherwise the leader knows he must coach Mr. Smith or devote more resources to the task, etc.

This type of accountability is often done at weekly meetings or special project meetings to ensure challenges are caught in time to correct issues before they become a problem.

As another example, I will share with you a portion of my actual strategic plan. I decided I wanted to increase my expert status and brand awareness.

That would be my overarching goal.

One of my strategic goals was to start a blog/newsletter with quality content.

The first action item was to compile all my databases, printed address, and business cards to one list.

I am a terrible typist (just ask my editor), so I knew I needed to outsource the data entry part of this task.

That action item would look like this:

> **A) Convert all 20,000 paper contacts to an excel spreadsheet.**
> Who: Nikki Jones   Start: Mar. 12, 2012
> Complete: Mar. 19, 2012 Outside cost $200

The second and third action items continue the process.

> **B) Research Mail Chimp, Constant Contact, Aweber and Go Daddy email marketing options.**
> Who: David Whitfield   Start: Mar. 15, 2012
> Complete: Mar. 25, 2012

C) Create a backlog of 10 articles to avoid not having content   during busy times or in case of emergencies.

Who: David Whitfield   Start: Mar. 15, 2012
Complete: Apr. 5, 2012

In this case, I delegated the data entry because it is not a good use of my time and, as I admitted, I am a horrid typist. I could have delegated the research of the email marketing options, but as I was going to be the principle user, I opted to do it myself. The creation of the content must be me; it is my credibility and expert status I am building.

You are the leader, so delegate what you can, and make sure you do what is most important.

Let's walk through the example above. If I (A) have the 20,000 names in a digital file, (B) import those names into an email program, and (C) have ten articles ready to publish, can I then start a blog/newsletter? Yes!

If I start a blog/newsletter with quality content will my brand awareness and expert status increase? I say YES!

As you can see, this simple, but effective, planning method creates a practical and easy to understand plan that sets an overarching goal. It is supported by strategic goals, and then brought to fruition with action items that are assigned to a particular person with a timeline for easy accountability.

The New Rule of Three

I hope you have enjoyed joining Bill on his journey and getting a glimpse of the power of The New Rule of Three. I want you to get as much value from the experience of reading this book as possible, so I have included the first article that started it all… *The New Rule of Three.*

Have you ever been overwhelmed by the enormity of a task you were given? Confused by the numerous aspects of a complex assignment? Do complicated situations demand complicated responses? I say the answer is as simple as 3, The Rule of Three.

The Rule of Three introduced itself to me in too many aspects of my life to ignore the application in today's business world. The first time I recall hearing The Rule of Three, although it was not named as such, was in the military. "When confronting an enemy," the gnarled old sergeant said, "how many sides do you want to attack from?" A room full of young Airman unanimously concluded that attacking from all four sides was the correct answer. The old sergeant shook his head and asked the simple question, "If you are trapped by the enemy what would you do?" Fight to the last man, we agreed. Now the sergeant said, "If you attack from three sides, you give the enemy a place to go." He headed off further questions by adding, "You control where they go, most likely into a position where they will be attacked from three sides."

The Rule of Three again made itself known to me in martial arts training. My instructor said, "You can overcome a larger, stronger opponent if you control timing, distance, and emotion." In martial arts, controlling distance and timing is accomplished by where you place yourself using distance, and the angle in which you face your opponent. Being at an odd distance and angle, you force your opponent to constantly adjust breaking his rhythm, timing, and overall effectiveness. You begin controlling emotions with your own; you master your fear or excitement to reach a state of calm. From a place of calm, you can taunt your opponent to anger him and keep him off balance. You can try and reason with them, or even stroke their ego to the point that the fight is no longer necessary in their mind.

During a recent marketing campaign, I began researching what successful businesses had in common. There were many things, but I should not have been surprised when three main topics surfaced again and again.

It was then that I named the phenomenon: The New Rule of Three. Simply put, when you identify the three most important factors in virtually any endeavor and concentrate on them, the majority of other smaller factors will fall into place.

The Rule of Three seemed to hold firm in business as it had in virtually every aspect of life. I set out to decide how best to help people succeed. I had to decide what the major factors of success in business were.

> Leadership (yours)
> Talent (in your people)
> and Marketing…
  …are the three in The Rule of Three for today's business.

Let's examine each in brief. First your leadership; as an owner or top-level manager, you must give clear instructions. You must set a course for employees to follow. There is quite a bit to leadership, you might say. I agree. But leadership itself is key. I teach a workshop on leadership to CEO's and top-tier managers, and these are the three major components: direction, communication, and motivation. These three actions, or actionable goals, set the stage for great leadership.

A leader must have and share the direction for their company and employees; they are the captain of the ship. For anyone to communicate a direction, they must know a few things. First, what they actually want out of life, their personal vision, a written explanation of a scene some years in the future. What the leader wants his life to look like, in say, 10 years. If in the vision is that he is spending 4 days a week with his family, he should begin to train someone to take over a large portion of his daily activities. If the vision dictates passing the business on to her child, there are a host of actions that she should begin to implement. As the name suggests, a personal vision is shared with precious few, but it should greatly affect everything the leader does in their planning.

Secondly, a leader must have a public vision. The vision is not fluff, but again, a picture of where the leader wants to take the business in a set amount of time. It should be made to include the scope you will achieve; will you be known statewide, nationally, or even globally? What will you be known for? Who will you help and how will you help them in the process? The public vision is shared with staff, vendors, customers, and everyone associated with the business. It is an inspiration and realistic picture of what is to come for the business.

With these two visions well in hand, the leader must create a strategic plan. Planning need not be complicated or as stressful as it is often thought of. Simply take the three parts of your public vision and ask what must happen for these things to occur. These will be your overarching goals. For each overarching goal, chose three strategies that will lead to its coming to fruition. Find for these strategies the three actions that must be taken for the completion of that strategy. It is a simple cause and effect; if the actions are taken, the strategies with be executed, and with the completion of the strategies, the overarching goals will be realized.

The formula holds true no matter the complexity of the objective. You may need more layers, but so long as you create actionable goals with the higher strategy in mind, you will achieve success. The simplicity of this planning method is perfect for accountability. Every goal and strategy can be given to a person or department, with a time table. The actionable goal demand a definitive answer to the question was this completed and when. It leaves no confusion as to who is responsible for each goal and allows for direct correction or celebration as warranted.

That CEO with a great plan that does not or cannot communicate that plan to his people will not have the support or buy-in that it takes to make the plan the profitable reality it could be. If the plan is communicated effectively and no one cares, it is equally as doomed. People that are motivated will give a well-communicated plan the benefit of the doubt and begin implementing their task in the larger context of the overall plan.

Celebration of a well-done task and effective completion of their aspect of the plan will keep staff working hard. The celebration becomes motivation, which breeds good work habits that lead to task completion, and quality work leads to celebration. The cycle continues to build on itself until everyone is incredibly motivated all the time. We all know the higher the motivation the greater the productivity.

The celebration need not be expensive or time-consuming. A thank you note written, not emailed, to the employee and the employee's boss or their bosses' boss, will have a drastic effect on moral. Throw out the old employee of the month plaque, $100 bonus, and parking space, and instead personalize a gift. A pair of Texans tickets to a sports fan or a subscription to Canoeing Today for the outdoor type will have a much great impact, and in some cases may be less expensive.

Using The Rule of Three, we have broken leadership down into three actionable goals: direction, communication, and motivation. These goals are easily set, and with simple follow-through, will have the desired effect of Leadership. In short, the organization is accomplishing the vision of the leaders and having a great time doing it.

Secondly, as Jim Collins points out in *Good to Great*, the right people are critically important to a company's growth and success. I named talent as the second in The Rule of Three for today's business. As you might imagine, I have three actionable items here as well.

First, chose the right people, the right talent. I am amazed that people would hire someone to head a department that represents 30% of their revenue, be that $10,000 or $10 million, but will not spend the relatively small amount of money on background checks or time doing a thorough check of references.

A client of mine confided in me that he had gone through over 100 applications and many interviews and had hired only two people. You might be thinking he must have been hiring for a CFO or other very important position.

You would be right - he was hiring for the front counter of his quick service restaurant. The cashiers are the hands and face of his business. By the way, he and the chain of which he is a part have been locally and nationally recognized for superior customer service for the last 13 years.

Secondly, well-trained talent (people) will maximize productivity as well. When I was an employee, my boss sent me to the Franklin Covey Time Management course. It was certainly an investment for him, the better use I made of my time the more I produced for him. A secondary benefit was a feeling of motivation at being given the opportunity to better myself. A few years ago, after turning that employer into my first client, I took his entire management staff to a Zig Ziglar motivational seminar.

The last key to keeping great talent can be found on every list ever published on the subject of 'Why do people leave a job?' The number one answer is always 'feeling unappreciated.' In some extreme cases, not feeling acknowledged at all. As a leader, you should be in a constant cycle of communicating with and motivating and celebrating your talent's productivity. If you follow that model, your people will never feel unappreciated.

Your three actionable goals for the two in The Rule of Three, talent, are to pick the right people, keep their skills and knowledge current, and show your appreciation.

These three activities will drastically improve the implementation of your vision and the plans created from it, and will insure the greatest opportunity for success.

Lastly, you must get the message about your great products and services to your best prospects. In other words…marketing.

Marketing holds a special place for me, as it was what started me in business; I learned early on that marketing had three distinct parts: the message, the target market, and the distribution method. The best crafted message that is delivered to the wrong people will yield nothing. Of course a great message, intended for the right target, which is never received due to poor placement, is equally worthless.

The right message is different for every business, but it must include your unique selling proposition; in short, it must say what you do better, faster, or cheaper than everyone else. It should be completely honest and have a call to action and all the possible ways prospects can find or get in touch with you; phone number, email, apps, and your website. If you have gotten their attention, make sure it is easy for them to buy from you.

Once you have crafted you message, you must carefully choose the target market you wish to reach. We all know that the top 20% of our clients provide us with 80% of our business, hence the 80/20 rule. I submit that you create a profile from only your top 20%. You choose how you define the top 20% - highest revenue, easiest to work with - however you define them. Once you know who they are, find out where they work, live, and play. Armed with that knowledge, you can determine the most productive distribution method, marketing to only those that fit the profile of your top 20%.

Any marketing campaign worth its salt will use different methods of getting the message to the intended prospects. Some of the most common are radio, television, direct mail, ad placement, and the often misused and maligned couponing. The key to great distribution is staying focused. Once you have identified your target market, you can select billboards in a small areas most frequented by your prospects or place ads in children's magazines, or have entries in holiday parades if your target is families in a certain geographic area.

Cable channels have made television advertising much more affordable and easier to focus by allowing you to select not only geographical area but the ability to purchase ads in programs tailored to the interest you identified as your target market.

There are many methods, and each business should explore many and test a few. Once you find those that effectively reach your focused target market, use them consistently; tweaking the message and offers to keep them fresh, and you will have effective marketing.

The implementation of The Rule of Three in business today, leadership, talent, and marketing, can simplify the complex and put straightforward actionable goals with great results easily within your reach.

May you achieve success as you define it!

David Whitfield

www.asaydi.com

Success as YOU Define it!

I believe the most important part of the New Rule of Three is Leadership. "Everything rises and falls on Leadership." – John C. Maxwell. The most important aspect of Leadership is creating a Private vision. So I have included my Personal Vision Worksheet. Please take the time to create this vision. It is the first step to… Success as YOU Define it!

When creating a Personal Vision we must address the whole person. To help us understand what or who "the whole person" is I have slightly adapted one of my hero's concepts. This of course is, based on Stephen Covey's Sharpen the Saw, the 7th Habit of Highly Successful People.

Physical/Material:	Beneficial eating, exercising, and resting. Having everything that you need and much of what you want.
Social/Emotional:	Making meaningful and social connections with friends and family.
Mental/Spiritual:	Learning, reading, writing, and teaching. Spending time in nature, expanding your spiritual self through meditation, music, art, prayer, or service.

When considering the subjects in the table below remember that the answer is in your perfect future vision. Do not let money or the "how you will get there" come into play. Just think big beautiful thoughts.

Physical/Material	Social/Emotional	Mental/Spiritual
Family Involvement Will it be Frank and Son's, will you have your daughter take over as CEO. How will your family be involved in your business if at all.	**Family Time** How much time do you want to spend with the family, a week or a year?	**Your Faith** How does your faith effect your business, having high ethical standards or like Dave Ramsey is it the core of everything
Total Family Benefits Does the employed spouse get a company car, is there a company boat for weekend use?	**Hobbies** What do you love to do…besides work...with your time	**Education** Go back and get that degree or upgrade to an MBA?
Four day work week Just how many days should be in your perfect workweek 1, 4 even 1/2?	**Stress** In your perfect vision what is your stress level, let's face it some of us thrive on stress	**Personal Growth** What challenges or improvement would you make in yourself as a person?
Net Worth If you don't know this one refer to the aforementioned Dave Ramsey.	**Personal Fulfillment** What have you done that fills you with joy and happiness on a deep personal level?	**Type of Business involvement** Are you hands on in the trenches kind of person or the check-in once a week CEO or something in between?
Personal Income (see net worth)	**Ego** We should admit it, most business people have egos. How has yours been satisfied how have you been recognized.	**Humanitarian** Is giving to your church or a great cause part of the perfect picture in your future?
Financial Risk Is your name off all the company loans and lines of credit or are you pouring more money into the next great idea?	**Political** Do you see yourself holding and office, helping a great candidate gets elected?	**Mental Outlook** On any given day is your attitude positive, excited, or relaxed.

What do you actually want out of life, choose at least 6 of the subjects on the previous page, stop now and highlight them. (It is ok to write in this book, I encourage it.)

These six or more things are the basis of your Personal Vision. The best way I found to be inspired by a vision is to create a written explanation of a scene some years in the future. What do you want your life to look like in say 10 years.

Choose a set event in the future. The child graduation, a birthday, anything that is memorable and on a fixed date. I will share with you my first Private Vision. I crafted it in 2005 a couple of years after my second daughter was born. Because it is a future I am working towards and I took time to really think about what would inspire me for the long term the vision's substance has not changed.

I return home form Meghan's graduation, where she graduated Cum-laude. I enter my 3500 square foot home and head to my office. I look over emails from my top account managers telling me we have helped another business owner reach their business and personal goals in other words "Achieve success as They defined it!". I put the finishing touches on Alyssa's Sunday school class lesson. I close down my state of the art computer and join my wife in her scrapbooking room to relax for the rest of the evening.

Please notice I did not use raw numbers to talk about my net worth or income. I used the size of my home and the state of the art computer to show I was doing well finically. I may add something about being debt free, I attended a Dave Ramsey EntreLeadership event yesterday (at the time of this writing) and he always make a good case for being debt free.

As for Family Time and Family Benefits I mentioned my daughter graduating Cum-laude. To me that expresses that I have given her both the time, knowledge and tools to achieve that lofty academic goal.

The idea of having a scrapbooking room my sound extravagant to some, great this is supposed to be an inspiring vision after all. To me it is more than one more room. Scrapebooking brings my mother, sister, wife and mother-in-law even my youngest daughter together for hours. That kind of extended family bonding is near priceless in this day and age.

Family and faith combine when I referred to preparing my preparing my youngest daughters Sunday school lesson. It speaks to my involvement not only with her (at seven they still like to have you around) but with my church as well.

Having a home office reminds me that I do not have to be in the office all the time. My top manager's messages of helping others brings to mind that, helping people succeed is the core of my business. The fact that only the top managers report to me directly reminds I am the CEO. It is easier to be a servant leader to people you do not directly supervise them. By the time you become one of my top manager our relationship is more one of collaboration than supervision. This separation allows me to work with the rest of my team in a less stressful atmosphere. Lastly simply relaxing with my wife shows a calm in my life and how much I value her and our relationship. As you can see I covered many of the subjects in the columns on our whole person chart. Physical/Material Social/Emotional Mental/Spiritual Careful consider those subjects you have highlighted.

Now choose a fixed event to serve as you date. It should be at least seven years away, so you have time to achieve big things. I find ten years serves well. Now start to write the story of where you will be at that time. It should be no less than 75 words but no more than 250 words. It needs to be short enough to think of and envisioned when ever life throws up an obstacle. Don't worry about appearing greedy or wanting to much. Shoot for the stars. The only people you will share this with already know you better than everyone else, you will not shock them.

Remember the purpose of the Private Vision is to be inspiring so go for it. You do not have to be a published author or English major, spelling and grammar do not matter. Write something that makes you go wow, I want to be there...today...right now! When you start to get envious of the future you, you probably have it.

I know some of you will insist that you cannot write or you cannot visualize. The Private Vision can be expressed in bullet statements...if you must.

In 2020...

I will be the CEO with a total compensation packaged of $300,000.

I will go sailing every other weekend and be stress free on the water.

I will sit on the City Council

 I will have a MBA I will lead a mission trip to build houses in Mexico

I will be spending 20 hours a week with my family

I will drive a new 1968 Candy Apple Red Corvette Convertible

It is of particular importance that you are very specific when using bullet statements as your Private vision. A Corvette is cool, a Candy Apple Red Corvette is awesome, but a 1968 Candy Apple Red Corvette Convertible, now that's inspiring.

Use the lines below to do a quick draft. You can type it up later. Remember this is for you, to inspire you. Someone else reading it need not understand it. The scrapbooking room, was very meaningful to me but its importance was likely not obvious when you read it. The few people you share this with, if any, should understand you enough to "get it" or you obviously trust them enough to explain it to them. One again…think big awesome thought. Write what will inspire you to power through lives obstacles.

_____

_____

_____

_____

_____

_____

_____

_____

Congratulations you have taken the first step to creating more time, decreasing stress and increasing productivity…the first step to …Achieving success as You define it!

I know this will serve you. If you want to inspire your team, your customers even vendors with a Public Vision…if you want to Simplify with strategies… If you would like to hire and keep the best people and have them happily working efficiently to make your vision a reality…

If you would like to discover or refocused on your Unique Spelling Proposition, create truly focused marketing messages and reach, sell and serve the perfect prospect…

If you would like to have more time, less stress and greater productivity please contact me at 832-266-9125, David@asaydi.com , or www.asaydi.com.

May you achieve success as You define it!

About the Author

As an International Speaker, I have had the honor of sharing information outside the US, in the UK, Japan and most recently China. I am an experienced writer and speaker in the fields of Experience Marketing, customer service, strategic planning and business growth. I have been heard on syndicated Radio, cable and broadcast television and published in The Houston Business Journal, the Houston Chronicle, Your Houston Business Magazine and several other newspapers and newsletters, as well as on online.

As the Principle Consultant for the firm I established, I was recognized and awarded for my work in the community and for my excellence in marketing and business. My first book, Beyond Service lies the Experience is currently offered on Amazon.com. My passion is Business Leadership and Focused Marketing!

With over twenty-five years of entrepreneurship, I developed a targeted program (direct mail, Email, and telephone follow-up) for a Technical Training school to promote certification and training for Dental Assistants. I created a direct mail piece; the Email copy; and wrote the script for the telephone follow-up. It generated a 75+% response rate and three full training classes within the first two weeks of the mail out. I created and implemented a comprehensive sales and marketing plan for four restaurants.

The program included, brand building, public relations, and community-related promotional events. As well as off-site catering as a new revenue stream. The plan increased year-over-year sales by 18% to 22% for a 10-year period.

As a John Maxwell Certified Coach, Trainer and Speaker, I can offer workshops, seminars, keynote speaking, and coaching; aiding your personal and professional growth through study and practical application of Maxwell's proven leadership methods. Working together, I will move you and/or your team or organization in the desired direction to reach your goals
.

Leadership is the difference maker and the deal breaker. It's how we grow organizations. It's how we impact lives. But, as you also know, leadership cannot be an idea we simply talk about. Leadership is the action we must live out.

A little more about me, I joined the United States Air Force; serving ten years in England, Japan, South Korea, the United Arab Emirates and the US, as a Security Police Officer. I have training and/or certification in: Strategic Business Leadership Coaching, Meeting Facilitation, Leadership School, TQM Level 1,2, and 3, The Karrass Effective Negotiating Class, Train the Trainer, Equal Opportunity Employer 2000, and The Franklin Covey Time Management Course.